TRACK MANAGEMENT

Check Lists for Track
Officials and Meet Managers

by
Andy Bakjian

APPROXIMATE METRIC EQUIVALENTS IN YARDAGE SYSTEM

1 Meter	—	39.37 inch
100 Meters	—	109 Yd., 1 Ft., 1 In.
110 Meters	—	120 Yd., 11 In.
200 Meters	—	218 Yd., 2 Ft., 2 In.
400 Meters	—	437 Yd., 1 Ft., 4 In.
800 Meters	—	874 Yd., 2 Ft., 8 In.
1500 Meters	—	1640 Yd., 1 Ft., 3 In.
3000 Meters	—	1 Mile, 1520 Yd., 2½ Ft.
3200 Meters	—	1 Mile, 1739 Yd., 1'8"
5000 Meters	—	3 Miles, 188 Yd., 2 In.
10000 Meters	—	6 Miles, 376 Yd., 4 In.
1 Inch	—	2.54 Centimeters
1 Foot	—	.0348 Meters
1 Yard	—	.9144 Meters
1 Mile	—	1609.3 Meters

CONTENTS

ABOUT THE AUTHOR

Andy Bakjian is currently Chairman of Officials for The Athletics Congress of the USA, the national governing body for track and field. His several decades of officiating experience, along with a stint as track coach at Jefferson High School in Los Angeles, have yielded practical guidelines for the beginning coach and/or official. As Andy puts it, *Track Management* is a "handbook compiled to assist the coach in the successful organization of a track meet. In short, Forget-Me-Nots." Though *Track Management* is geared toward larger invitational or championship meets and toward big-school track programs, the book is useful for putting on meets at all levels. In many cases, Bakjian presents the ideal situation re number of officials, track managers, etc. The reader must scale down to fit his situation and available personnel. Though many rules are referred to throughout the book, the reader is urged to refer at all times to the rulebook governing his particular meet, association, etc.

ACKNOWLEDGEMENTS

The publishers would like to thank Wilkins International for permission to use the schematic of a 400-meter track. Reproduction of this schematic may not be done without the written permission of Wilkins International, 1145 Rolling Green Dr., Waukesha, WI 53186.

SEEDING AND LANE DRAW

Method I (This procedure is used in many dual meets.)

The track coaches from both schools who will meet that week will agree which school will have the "odd" or the "even" events.

When this is done, the track coaches will list the athletes from that school on the recording event sheets in every other lane in each event or heat.

Method II

The track coaches will draw by lot and then place the athletes in the lanes that correspond to the number drawn. (Many times track coaches will let their athletes draw their own numbers.)

Method III

The track coaches accept the times the athletes have recorded in previous track meets and then place the two fastest runners in the middle lanes in the sprints and hurdles and place the other runners according to their times in the other lanes.

In longer races, the best time is placed on the pole position. The rest of the runners are placed in the other lanes.

Method IV

If more than one heat; The Games Committee will draw by lot each heat.

They can also place runners in heats according to their best performances in previous meets.

(The same procedure is used for the field events; if not done by lot, the usual method is to place the athlete with the worst mark first, then in ascending order, with the athlete with the best previous mark throwing or jumping last.)

TIME SCHEDULE EXAMPLES

DUAL MEET PACIFIC-10

Long Jump . . . . 1:15 P.M.
Pole Vault . . . . 1:15 P.M.

Shot Put . . . . .1:30 P.M.
Javelin Throw . . . . .1:30 P.M.
High Jump. . . . . .1:45 P.M.
400 Meter Relay . . . . .2:00 P.M.
3000 Meter Steeplechase. . . . . .2:10 P.M.
1500 Meter Run . . . . .2:25 P.M.
110 Meter High Hurdles .2:35 P.M.
400 Meter Dash. . . . . .2:45 P.M.
100 Meter Dash. . . . . .2:55 P.M.
800 Meter Run . . . . .3:05 P.M.
400 Meter Intermediate Hurdles . . . . .3:15 P.M.
200 Meter Dash. . . . . .3:25 P.M.
5000 Meter Run . . . . .3:35 P.M.
Mile Relay. . . . . .3:55 P.M.

Discus Throw . . . . .Follows the Shot Put and Javelin Throw.

Triple Jump. . . . . .Follows the Long Jump.

HIGH SCHOOL TRACK AND FIELD
(MEN AND WOMEN)

Start Field Events at 1:30 P.M.

1:30 P.M.	Pole Vault	— "C" Division	(Men)
1:30 P.M.	High Jump	— Women	
1:30 P.M.	Shot Put	— "C" Division	(Men)
		Varsity	(Men)
1:30 P.M.	Long Jump	— Varsity	(Men)
		Women	
2:00 P.M.	Pole Vault	— "B" Division	(Men)
		Varsity	(Men)
2:00 P.M.	High Jump	— "B" Division	(Men)
		Varsity	(Men)
2:00 P.M.	Shot Put	— "B" Division	(Men)
		Women	
2:00 P.M.	Long Jump	— "B" and "C" Division	(Men)
2:30 P.M.	Triple Jump	— Varsity	(Men)

Track Events:

2:30 P.M.	800 Meter Sprint Medley Relay	— Women	
2:35 P.M.	120 Meter High Hurdles	— Varsity	(Men)
2:40 P.M.	70 Meter High Hurdles	— "B" Division	(Men)

2:45 P.M.	1500 Meter Run	— "C" Division	(Men)
2:55 P.M.	400 Meter Relay	— Varsity	(Men)
3:00 P.M.	400 Meter Relay	— Women	
3:05 P.M.	800 Meter Run	— Varsity	(Men)
3:10 P.M.	800 Meter Run	— Women	
3:15 P.M.	100 Meter Dash	— "C" Division	(Men)
3:20 P.M.	100 Meter Dash	— "B" Division	(Men)
3:25 P.M.	100 Meter Dash	— Varsity	(Men)
3:30 P.M.	100 Meter Dash	— Women	
3:35 P.M.	1500 Meter Run	— Varsity	(Men)
3:40 P.M.	1500 Meter Run	— Women	
3:50 P.M.	800 Meter Run	— "C" Division	(Men)
3:55 P.M.	800 Meter Run	— "B" Division	(Men)
4:00 P.M.	400 Meter Run	— Varsity	(Men)
4:05 P.M.	400 Meter Run	— Women	
4:10 P.M.	120 Meter Run	— "C" Division	(Men)
4:15 P.M.	120 Meter Low Hurdles	— "B" Division	(Men)
4:20 P.M.	110 Meter Low Hurdles	— Women	
4:25 P.M.	330 Meter Low Hurdles	— Varsity	(Men)
4:30 P.M.	200 Meter Dash	— "C" Division	(Men)
4:35 P.M.	200 Meter Dash	— "B" Division	(Men)
4:40 P.M.	200 Meter Dash	— Varsity	(Men)
4:45 P.M.	200 Meter Dash	— Women	
4:50 P.M.	1500 Meter Run	— "B" Division	(Men)
5:00 P.M.	3000 Meter Run	— Varsity (Men) and Women	
5:20 P.M.	400 Meter Relay	— "C" Division	(Men)
5:25 P.M.	400 Meter Relay	— "B" Division	(Men)
5:30 P.M.	1600 Meter Relay	— Women	
5:35 P.M.	1600 Meter Relay	— Varsity	(Men)

GENERAL GUIDELINES FOR OFFICIALS

Necessary items and rules for Track and Field Officials:

1. *A Red Flag and a White Flag.* The red flag is waved to indicate that a foul was committed or for an unsuccessful attempt. The white flag is waved to indicate that a legal or successful attempt was completed. It is also used to indicate that the official is ready.

2. *Stop Watch.* Schools should purchase good stopwatches, a Chronomix and if affordable, an automatic Photo-Timer.

3. *Clip-Board, Pencils or Pens.* Each official should have these items when he arrives at the meet site.

4. *Measuring Tapes.* Feet and Metric Steel Tapes—3.0 meters (10 feet), 7.6 meters (25 feet), 30.48 meters (100 feet), 45.76 meters (150 feet), 91.44 meters (300 feet).

5. *Plasticine (Horizontal Jump Officials).* This is spread on the inner edge (toward the pit) of the toe-board to check foot-faults in the Long and Triple Jumps.

6. *Report to the Head Official* of your assigned event as soon as you arrive at the track site. (It is recommended that the official arrive at least 30 minutes before the event is to begin).

7. *Do not leave the area of your assigned event* (e.g., to go to the rest room or to get a drink of water) unless you check with the Head Official of your event).

8. *Prepare and be knowledgeable of the rules* involving your assigned event. Refer to the rule book that pertains to that particular track meet.

    a) National Federation of State High School Associations.
    b) The Athletics Congress/U.S.A.
    c) International Amateur Athletic Federation.
    d) National Collegiate Athletic Association.
    e) National Association of Intercollegiate Athletics (uses NCAA book).
    f) Association for Intercollegiate Athletics for Women.

    g)   National Junior College Athletic Association
        (uses NCAA book).

9. *Check the event recording sheet* on how to record each
   trial, such as, for the vertical jumps:

        "O" = Fair or successful attempt.
        "X" = Foul or unsuccessful attempt.
        "-" = Passed his trial attempt.
        (New I.A.A.F. Rule: A passed trial attempt means
        the competitor passes that height completely).

10. *When your event has been completed, check with the
    Head Official* of your event before you leave the area.

STEEPLECHASE ORGANIZATION

The water jump in the 3000-meter Steeplechase may be located inside or outside the regular track. In either case, however, the contestants must clear 28 hurdles and 7 water jumps during the course of the race.

Since the inside-the-track set-up is most common, here are the figures/distances for this arrangement:

The runners will first cover 270 meters without a jump, then they will run 7 laps of 390 meters each, each of the 7 laps having 5 barriers or hurdles, including one water jump. (270m + [7 x 390m] = 3000m.) The distance between each hurdle (including the water jump) is 78m.

Hurdles Number 3 and 5 (see diagram) are kept off the track until the runners have passed those points on their first circuit of the track.

SPECIFICATIONS OF HURDLES AND WATER JUMP

Each hurdle is 3 feet (.914 meters) high, with a plus or minus 3mm tolerance. The hurdle is 13 feet wide (3.96 meters) minimum at the top bar. The hurdle is placed so that the top bar extends 1 foot inside the field. The top bar section is 127mm (5") square.

The water jump is 3.66 meters (12 feet) square, 70 cm. (2 feet, 3½ inches) deep at the end nearest the hurdle, sloping to ground level at the farthest end. The hurdle height is the same as the other hurdles. Matting, or some suitable protective material to ensure safe landing of the runners, should be placed at the farthest end of the jump (2.5 meters long by 3.66 meters wide).

WHERE STEEPLECHASE INSPECTORS SHOULD BE STATIONED

Number 1 and 2 Inspectors check the runners as they come down the straightaway and go into the curve.

Number 2 and 3 Inspectors check the runners coming around the curve and to the hurdle jump.

Number 4 Inspector watches the runners coming to the hurdle jump and the back-stretch.

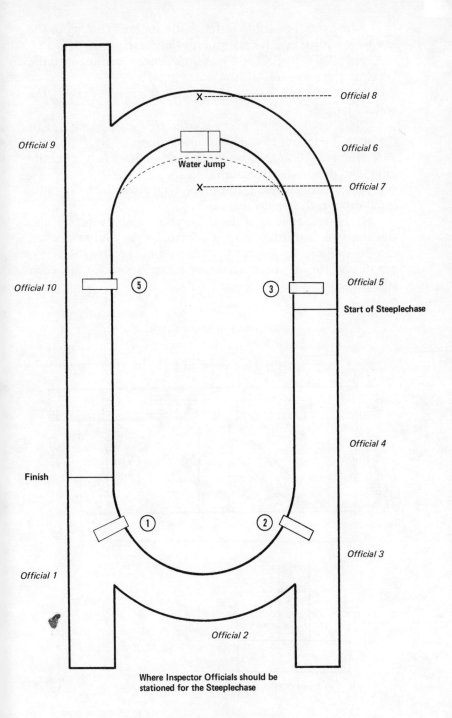

Where Inspector Officials should be
stationed for the Steeplechase

Number 5 Inspector watches the runners coming to the hurdle jump and when they go into the curve.

Number 6 Inspector checks the runners coming into the curve and heading toward the water jump.

Number 7 and 8 Inspectors watch the runners taking the water jump.

Number 9 Inspector checks the runners coming out of the water jump and to the next hurdle jump.

Number 10 Inspector checks the runners to the hurdle jump and down the straightaway.

Inspectors watch for trailing leg infractions, and the usual other race infractions.

It is recommended to assign ten inspectors for the steeplechase, but if ten are not available, then four inspectors can be assigned to inspect the curves and the straightaways, one inspector at each curve and one inspector at each straightaway.

STEEPLECHASE HURDLE DIMENSIONS

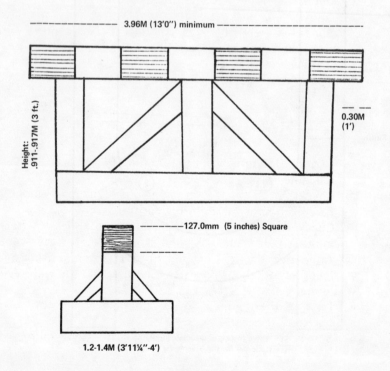

3.96M (13'0") minimum

Height: .911-.917M (3 ft.)

0.30M (1')

127.0mm (5 inches) Square

1.2-1.4M (3'11¼"-4')

-8-

HIGH JUMP

EQUIPMENT

1. *Standards:* It is the responsibility of the home school or meet director to verify that the high jump standards are in good working order.
2. *Crossbar:* The crossbar shall be straight and officially colored, triangular or circular in shape, and the tips that rest on the supports shall be smooth.
3. *Stop Watch:* An official will be in charge of timing so the competitor will not exceed the 1-½ minutes allotted time to complete his/her jump after name has been called.
4. *Broom:* A broom is necessary to keep the high jump apron clean for the competitors.
5. *Chairs:* High jump officials should be seated when the competitor is ready to jump.
6. *Landing Pit:* Make sure the landing pit does not have any foreign objects on it, and also check that it is well placed and secure.
7. *Competitors Bench.*
8. *Name Indicator Board.*

HEAD HIGH JUMP OFFICIAL

1. Arrive at least one hour before the high jump is scheduled to begin.
2. Check the standards, crossbars, landing mats and the take-off boards for any irregularities.
3. Check in the high jump competitors at least fifteen minutes before the schduled starting time of the event.
4. Announce the starting height to the competitors and record the height at which each competitor will begin jumping.
5. Line up the competitors in "jumping order" for introductions, if needed.
6. Supervise the measurement of each height in meters

(and feet for those who do not understand the metric system).

7. Inform the competitors in advance that you are invoking the "Time Limit Rule" (1-½ minutes) for a trial and make sure the competitor knows when the time is to begin.

8. Determine and inform the competitor whether the trial jump was successful or unsuccessful according to the rules of the event.

9. Never lower the crossbar once competition has started (except for jump-offs).

10. Assign the assistant high jump officials to their positions.

11. Assign an official to keep the area clear of spectators.

12. Enforce the rule about where markings on the high jump approach can be placed by competitors.

13. Determine the finishing place and height of each competitor at the end of the competition and affix your signature to the event card. Distribute results as required.

14. Return all equipment to the proper place.

ASSISTANT HIGH JUMP OFFICIALS

1. Arrive at least 45 minutes before the high jump is scheduled to begin.

2. Assist the Head Official in lining up the competitors for introductions.

3. Assist (when requested) in the measurements of the heights.

4. Replace the crossbar properly after each missed attempt or at a new height. The smooth sides of the crossbar tips are placed on the high jump standard bars. The same side should always be up.

5. Assist in determining whether a jump is successful or unsuccessful.

6. Check the results of competition as tabulated by the Head Official.

7. Remeasure the winning height.

8. Competitors have 1-½ minutes allotted time to complete their trial jumps when their names are called.

9. Do not talk to the competitors or any one of the officials when a competitor is ready to jump.

HELPFUL HINTS FOR THE HIGH JUMP OFFICIALS

1. High Jump standards should not be less than 3.66 meters (12 feet) or more than 4.02 meters (13 feet 2-½ inches apart.
2. Take-off surface must be level.
3. Approach surface should be not less than 21.3 meters (70 feet).
4. Announce the heights to the competitors.
5. Measurements shall be made from the ground to the lowest part of the upper side of the crossbar with a certified steel tape or bar.
6. A new height shall be measured before the competitors can attempt such a height.
7. It is advisable to check the measurement of the crossbar after each successful or unsuccessful trial.
8. Replace the crossbar with the same surface up and the same surface facing the front.
9. Competitor may place a marker on his "run-up" and "take-off."
10. Three (3) consecutive failures eliminate a competitor from further competition.
11. The Referee is the only authorized person who is allowed to move the uprights if he feels the "take-off" and the landing area have become unsatisfactory.
12. Never lower the crossbar once competition has started (except for jump-offs).
13. High jump competitors may be allowed to jump out of order, if competing in another event going on at the same time. (True for other field events, as well.)
14. High Jump and Pole Vault are normally scored as follows:
     "O" = Successful attempt
     "X" = Unsuccessful attempt
     "-" = Pass
NOTE: New IAAF rule indicates that a pass any time means that the competitor passes the height completely. An athlete, for instance, cannot pass his first attempt at a given height, then take his second attempt; he must wait until the next height.

OFFICIALS STATIONED FOR THE HIGH JUMP

Officials Number 1 (Head) and 2 are seated at least six (6) feet on each side of the high jump standards. Official 1 will have a red and white flag. He will wave the red flag indicating that the jump was not successful and will wave the white flag indicating that the jump was a successful jump.

Number 1 and 2 will set the bar at the correct heights and will check measurements.

Officials Numbers 3 and 4 will keep the area behind the landing mats clear of spectators and assist in adjusting the landing mats when needed.

Official Number 5 will keep the event sheet and record the jumps as fair, foul or passed. This Official will work closely with Officials 1 and 2. He will also keep the time so the competitor will not exceed the 1-and-½ minutes allowed to complete his jump after his name has been called. This official must have a stop watch.

Officials Number 6 and 7 will keep the area behind the competitors clear of spectators.

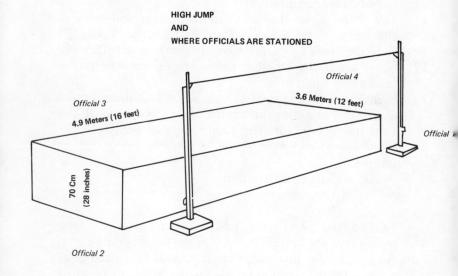

HIGH JUMP
AND
WHERE OFFICIALS ARE STATIONED

Official 4

Official 3

3.6 Meters (12 feet)

4.9 Meters (16 feet)

Official

70 Cm (28 inches)

Official 2

Official 6

Official 5

Official 7

THE BREAKING OF TIES IN THE FIELD EVENTS

High   Jump and Pole Vault.
1. Competitor with the lowest number of jumps at the height at which the tie occurs is the winner.
2. If tie is not settled, then it is decided by the lowest number of failures throughout the competition.
3. If ties still remains, then each competitor gets another attempt at the height at which the tie occurred. If both are successful, the bar is raised one-inch in the high jump, three inches in the pole vault, or lowered the same amounts in case both are unsuccessful, continuing in this manner until the tie is resolved. This is known as a jump-off. A jump-off is only conducted for first place.

Other Field Events:
Ties are broken by referring to the competitors' second-best marks. If still tied, refer to the third-best marks, and so on.

POLE VAULT

EQUIPMENT

1. *Pole Vault Standards:* Pole vault standards should be in good working order. Check the base, bar pins and how well the measuring poles slide up and down. Also confirm that the sliding poles lock firmly.
2. *Crossbar:* The crossbar should be straight and officially colored. The end tips must be smooth and should not have any adhesive substance on them.
3. *Crossbar Replacement Device:* This piece of equipment is necessary and very important to have on hand. It saves a great deal of time if you can appoint a good crossbar replacer.
4. *Landing Pit:* The landing pit should be well placed and belted together.
5. *Vaulting Pole Rack:* This item should be placed outside the restraining ropes. Vaulting poles should not be lying around on the ground.
6. *Ladder:* Have a 15 foot ladder available to measure the height of the bar when it becomes officially necessary.
7. *Stop Watch:* One official will officially keep time on each vaulter's jump. The vaulter must not exceed the two minute time that is allotted to him to complete his trial after his name has been called. It is also recommended one have a large stop clock (digital preferred) so vaulters can check the time remaining.
8. *Broom:* It is advisable to keep the runway clean.
9. *Name Indicator Boards:* The home school or meet director is responsible for furnishing these items and should also assign a knowledgeable person to operate the standards.
10. *Bench for the Competitors:* A bench should be placed to the side of the runway so the vaulters who are not competing may be seated.
11. *Measuring tape—25 ft.*

A suitable pole vault landing pit is 5 x 5 meters (16 feet, 4 inches square). It should contain foam rubber and should be at least three feet high.

The runway is at least 38.1 meters long (125 feet) and 1.22 meters wide.

The pole vault planting box must be of legal size.

The standards are placed at least 3.66 meters (12 feet) and not more than 4.37 meters (14 feet, 4 inches) apart at the front edges of the landing pit and are adjustable to 5.5 meters (18 feet) or more in height.

The crossbar is made of wood or metal or fiberglass.

The pole is of unlimited size and weight. Each vaulter furnishes his own poles and a vaulter, naturally, must not use another vaulter's pole without receiving permission from the owner.

HEAD POLE VAULT OFFICIAL

1. Arrive at least 45 minutes before the pole vault is scheduled to begin and check the pole vault implements, equipment, crossbar, poles, and the tape on the poles.
2. Pick up the pole vault recording sheets.
3. Assign the Assistant Vault Officials to their stations.
4. Check in the vaulters and explain the order of competition to them, the starting height and subsequent intervals.
5. Review the rules with the Assistant Pole Vault Officials before the competition begins.
6. Line up the competitors for introductions, if needed.
7. Have each vaulter take his turn in order and without delaying the event. Vaulter has two minutes to complete his trial from the time his name is called.
8. Check tabulation of the place winners, and order of finish.
9. Certify results and distribute as required.
10. Return equipment to the proper place.

ASSISTANT POLE VAULT OFFICIALS

1. Arrive at least thirty minutes before the pole vault event is scheduled to begin and report to the Head Pole Vault Official and receive your assignment.
2. Assist the Head Pole Vault Official in checking the equipment and all the necessary items that pertain to the pole vault event.

3. Check the vaulting poles for proper wrapping (no more than two wraps of tape at the grip end).
4. Competitors must be properly uniformed.
5. Judge and record each attempt of each vaulter.
6. Catch the pole of each vaulter if it is falling away from the landing pit.
7. Make sure the crossbar is placed on the pegs with the same part facing the front.
8. It is permissible for the pole to go under the bar in a successful attempt.
9. In case of a record, two pole vault officials, the Head Field Official and the Referee shall witness the measurement of the height of the crossbar before and after the successful attempt.
10. Have each vaulter take his turn in order and not delay the event. The vaulter has two minutes allotted time to complete the jump when the Pole Vault Official calls out the competitor's name.
11. Work closely with the Head Pole Vault Official.
12. Help keep the landing pit and runway areas clear of spectators.
13. When the pole vault has concluded, assist in returning the equipment to the storage shack.

HELPFUL HINTS FOR POLE VAULT OFFICIALS

1. Competitor is not allowed to move his lower hand above the upper hand or move the upper hand higher on the pole after leaving the ground in an attempt.
2. Measurements should be made with a steel tape or bar graduated in quarter inches and/or centimeters.
3. All new heights shall be measured.
4. In an attempt to establish a record, the height of the crossbar must be measured before and after the attempt.
5. Replace the crossbar with the same upper surface and the same front surface.
6. No marks are to be placed on the runway, but a marker or markers may be placed alongside the runway.
7. Competitor may, at his own discretion, commence vaulting at the starting height or any subsequent height.
8. Competitors may have the uprights moved forward or back, but may not move them more than 2 feet.
9. When the uprights are moved, remeasurement shall be made.

10. Ends of the crossbar shall not project more than .15 meters (6 inches).
11. Competitors are permitted to use adhesive substance on their hands and poles, but may not wear gloves.
12. See High Jump section for scoring and tie-breaking guidelines.

AN UNSUCCESSFUL ATTEMPT HAS OCCURRED IF THE COMPETITOR:

1. Knocks the crossbar off the pegs with the pole or body;
2. Leaves the ground for the purpose of making a vault and fails to clear the bar;
3. After leaving the ground, places the lower hand above the upper hand or moves the upper hand higher;
4. Touches beyond the vertical plane with his body or pole;
   or
5. If the official touches the pole when it is falling toward the bar or uprights, if in the opinion of the Head Pole Vault Official the bar would have been dislodged.

HINTS ABOUT BASIC RULES IN THE POLE VAULT:

1. It is not a foul if the pole passes underneath the crossbar in a successful attempt.
2. It shall not count as an attempt if the pole breaks during the attempt.
3. Pole may be of any length or combination of materials.
4. Pole may be of any length or diameter.
5. Pegs on the uprights are to be round, uniform thickness and not more than 76.2 millimeters (3 inches) long.
6. Landing pits should measure not less than 5 meters (16 feet 4 inches) square.
7. There is no restriction to taping the bottom end of the pole for a length of 1 foot.
8. The crossbar should be replaced with the same surface up and the same surface facing front.

WHERE POLE VAULT OFFICIALS
SHOULD BE STATIONED

Six Officials can adequately officiate the pole vault. Number 1 (Head) and 2 Officials: They are seated at least 6 feet away from the pole vault standards. One Official is seated on each side of the pole vault standards. Each

POLE VAULT

AND

WHERE OFFICIALS AND WORKING CREW ARE STATIONED

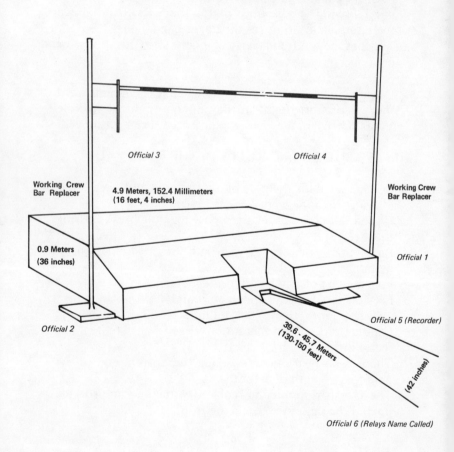

Official 3

Official 4

Working Crew
Bar Replacer

4.9 Meters, 152.4 Millimeters
(16 feet, 4 inches)

Working Crew
Bar Replacer

0.9 Meters
(36 inches)

Official 1

Official 2

39.6 - 45.7 Meters
(130-150 feet)

Official 5 (Recorder)

(42 inches)

Official 6 (Relays Name Called)

Official is responsible for catching the pole if it is falling away from the landing pit. These officials will also be responsible for setting the crossbar correctly and checking measurements. They also look for infractions by competitors.

Number 3 and 4 Officials: They are seated at least 10 feet behind the landing pit to keep that area clear of spectators. They also make sure the landing pit is in good position for the next vaulter.

Number 5 Official: He is seated most of the time and records each vault as: "X" = Foul, "O" = Fair and "-" = Passed. As soon as he records the result, he calls for the next vaulter.

Number 6 Official: This official relays the call to the competitors' bench to make sure the next vaulter has heard the call. He may also time the vaulter.

The vaulter has 2 minutes to complete his vault after his name has been called.

FIELD EVENT RECORDING SHEET
HIGH JUMP - POLE VAULT

EVENT NO. _____   MEET _____
TOTAL ENTRIES _____   DATE _____
FLIGHTS _____   PLACE _____
NO. OF PLACES _____   MEET RECORD _____

COMPETITOR	NO.	AFFILIATION	MEASURED HEIGHT																	BEST HEIGHT		METRIC HEIGHT
																				FEET	INCHES	

PRESS COPY

LONG JUMP

EQUIPMENT

1. *Measuring Tape*, 15.2 Meters (50 feet).
2. *Shovels (pointed and broad-nosed).*
3. *Leveling Board.*
4. *Side-line Tape*, 45.6 Meters (150 feet).
5. *Rake* (2 are sufficient).
6. *Broom.*
7. *Chairs.*
8. *Name Indicator Board.*
9. *Bench for Competitors.*
10. *Stop Watch* (large type so the competitor can see the time).
11. *Plasticine.*
12. *Fair/foul flags* (white and red).

The long-jump pit is 2.75 meters (9 feet) wide and it is approximately 6.4 meters (21 feet) long. It contains sand.

The runway is at least 40 meters (131 feet) long and 4 feet wide and it is dirt or of all-weather material. The top of the landing pit is to be level with the take-off board which is of standard dimensions.

The take-off board is not more than 3.6 meters (12 feet) from the edge of the pit and shall not be less than 10.0 meters (33 feet) from the rear edges. The take-off board shall be 8 inches wide and 1.21-1.22 meters (4 feet) long and shall be made normally of wood and painted white.

LONG JUMP CHECKLIST

1. *The take-off board* must be well embedded and level with the ground and landing pit.
2. *Measuring Tapes:* 50 foot and a 150 foot steel measuring tapes will be adequate. The 150 foot tape should be stretched along the side of the runway before the competition so athletes can find their marks. Metric tapes are normally required.
3. *Shovels:* Have two shovels (a broad-nose and a pointed-nose). These items are necessary to fill in the holes in

the pit made by the jumpers.

4. *Hard Tooth Rake:* After the holes have been filled, a member of the working crew can level and smooth the pit.

5. *Level Board:* When the shovel and rake crews have completed their jobs, the level crew (3 attendants) can level the landing pit, using the level board.

6. *Broom:* It is necessary to have a broom to keep the runway and take-off board clean.

7. *Stop Watch.* It is advisable for one of the officials to have a stop watch to check the time that is allotted for the jumper to complete his jump. It is also recommended that a large clock (preferably digital) be available and placed near the runway so the competitor can also check his allotted time of 1½ minutes to complete his jump.

8. *Chairs:* Long jump officials should be seated when the competitor is ready to jump.

9. *Name and Jump Mark Standards:* This is the responsibility of the home school or stadium. The school should assign an attendant to operate each one of the standards.

10. *Bench:* A bench should be placed near the start of the runway so those long jump competitors who are not competing may be seated.

HEAD LONG JUMP OFFICIAL

1. Arrive at least 45 minutes before the long jump is scheduled to begin.
2. Check the runway, take-off board, sand-pit, equipment and all items that will be needed for the safety of the competitors and the officials.
3. Pick up the Long Jump Recording Event card from the Head Field Official. Inform athletes as to order of jumping.
4. Assign the assistant long jump officials to their areas.
5. Make sure that there is enough plasticine or other suitable material for foul detection available.
6. Start the event as scheduled.
7. Line up the competitors for introductions, if needed.
8. Check shoe spikes for use on an all-weather runway.

9. Keep the area clear of spectators and non-competitors.
10. At the conclusion of the preliminaries, certify which competitors qualify for the finals.
11. Certify the results when the event is concluded and have them distributed to the proper individuals.
12. Make sure all equipment is returned to the proper place.

ASSISTANT LONG JUMP OFFICIALS

1. Arrive at least 30 minutes before the long jump is scheduled to begin and get your assignment (from the Head Long Jump Official.)
2. Make sure the working crew has the landing pit smooth and level for each competitor.
3. Help keep the area clear of spectators and non-competing athletes.
4. Measure the jumps from the front end of the take-off board to the break in the sand nearest to the take-off board. Break is made by any part of the competitor's foot, hand or body.
5. Record measurements to the lowest ¼ inch or centimeter.
6. Make sure the larger digital clock (if available) is set for each competitor when his name is called to compete. Each athlete has 1½ minutes to complete his jump.

HELPFUL HINTS FOR LONG JUMP OFFICIALS

1. Record and circle the best jumps of each competitor.
2. The plasticine should not be thicker than 10-13mm.
3. Fouls:
   a) If the competitor touches beyond the take-off board (and leaves a visible impression on the plasticine).
   b) The competitor touches the ground outside the pit.
   c) Walks back through the pit area after a completed trial.
   d) Somersaults.
   e) Uses weights or grips of any kind to aid in jumping.
4. No marks are allowed on the runway or in the landing-pit. They are allowed beside the runway.

WHERE LONG JUMP OFFICIALS
SHOULD BE STATIONED

Number 1 (Head) and 2 Officials: Each official is seated at least 6 feet from each side of the take-off board. They check for the legality of the jumps and wave the white flag for fair, red for foul jumps.

Number 3 and 4 Officials: These officials are also seated at least 6 feet from each side of the landing pit. Both of them check the mark the jumper has made in the landing pit. Number 3 Official, using a straight rod, sticks it in the rear part of the mark the jumper has made in the landing pit. Number 4 Official, who is in charge of the measuring tape in the landing pit, holds the tip of the measuring tape next to the rod.

Number 5 and 6 Officials: They keep the rear of the landing-pit clear of spectators.

Number 7 Official: He is seated and records the measured jumps on the event sheet. When all long jump officials are ready, the Number 7 Official will call out the name of the next competitor. The competitor must not exceed the 1½ minute time rule that is allotted to him to complete his jump.

Number 8 Official: This official relays the name of the competitor to make sure that the competitor is aware that his name has been called.

Working Crew: The shovel, rake and level crews take over as soon as the officials have completed measuring the jump.

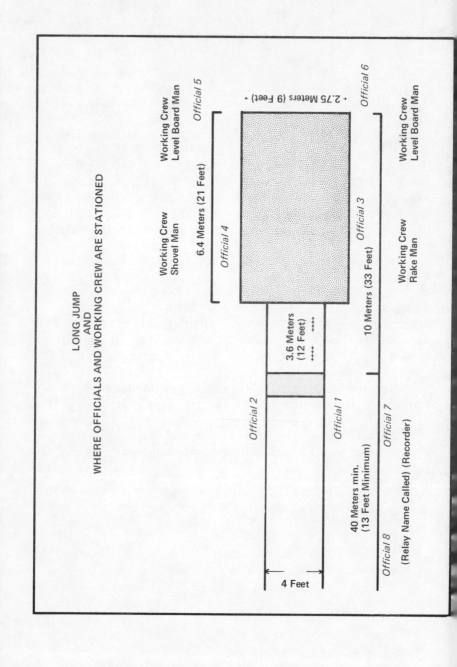

LONG JUMP
AND
WHERE OFFICIALS AND WORKING CREW ARE STATIONED

Working Crew Level Board Man
Official 5

← 2.75 Meters (9 Feet) →

Working Crew Shovel Man

6.4 Meters (21 Feet)

Official 4

Official 2

3.6 Meters (12 Feet)

Official 3

10 Meters (33 Feet)

Official 1

Working Crew Level Board Man
Official 6

Working Crew Rake Man

Official 7

Official 8

40 Meters min. (13 Feet Minimum)

(Relay Name Called) (Recorder)

4 Feet

-24-

TRIPLE JUMP

EQUIPMENT

1. *Measuring Tape*—150 feet.
2. *Level Board.*
3. *Rake and Shovel.*
4. *Broom.*
5. *Chairs for Officials.*
6. *Bench for the Competitors.*
7. *Name Indicator Board.*
8. *Plasticine.*
9. *Fair/foul flags* (white and red).

THE TRIPLE JUMP CHECK LIST

1. *Take-Off Board* is to be painted white.
2. *Measuring Tapes:* The measuring tapes should be steel tapes. One tape, 100 feet, is used for measuring the jump and the other, 150 feet, is stretched along the side of the runway so the competitors can mark their check-marks.
3. *Landing-Pit:* Specifications are the same as in the Long Jump.
4. *Foul/Fair Flags:* The Number 1 and 2 Officials are responsible for indicating the foul and fair jumps.
5. *Level Board Crew:* The home school should assign three qualified students to handle the level board.
6. *Rake, Shovels and Broom:* One person is assigned to each one of the items listed.
7. *Chairs:* All triple jump officials are to be seated when the competitor is ready to compete.
8. *Stop Watch and Digital Clock:* One of the assistant officials will keep the allotted time for each competitor. A large digital clock, if available, should also indicate the time the competitor has remaining to complete his jump.
9. *Bench:* A bench should be provided so the triple jump competitors may be seated when they are not competing.

HEAD TRIPLE JUMP OFFICIAL

1. Follow the same procedure as the Head Long Jump Official.
2. Make sure the measuring tape is of steel or fiberglass. Metric tape is normally required.
3. Check how much plasticine is available.
4. Examine the triple jump boards for security.
5. Meet with the assistant triple jump officials and instruct them on the rules and regulations of the triple jump.
6. Assign the assistant triple jump officials to their areas.
7. Brief competitors and notify them of the jumping order.
8. Line up the competitors for introductions, if needed.
9. When the event has been concluded, certify the results and distribute as required.
10. Make sure all equipment is returned to the proper place.

ASSISTANT TRIPLE JUMP OFFICIALS

1. Operate in the same manner as Assistant Long Jump Officials.
2. Carry out your assignment to the best of your ability as assigned by the Head Triple Jump Official.
3. Assist the other triple jump officials when needed.

HELPFUL HINTS FOR TRIPLE JUMP OFFICIALS

1. Keep the runway clear and clean.
2. Competitor must land first on the same foot that he took off on (hop); in the step phase, he lands on the other foot.
3. It is a foul if the trailing or "sleeping" leg touches the ground.
4. Measure all fair jumps with a steel tape.
5. Be professional in your assignment.

WHERE OFFICIALS SHOULD BE STATIONED

All triple jump officials and the working crew are seated when the competitor is ready to compete.

Officials Number 1 (Head) and 2 are seated, one on each side of the toe-board, and they check for foul and fair jumps.

The red flag is waved by the Number 2 Official indicating that the jump was foul, but if the jump was fair, then he would wave the white flag. They also handle the measuring tape at the take-off board, relaying the marks to Official Number 6.

Officials Number 3 and 4 check the mark made by the jumper in the landing pit. The Number 3 Official will stake the mark with the measuring rod.

As soon as the measurement has been submitted to the Number 6 Official for recording, the working crew will get the landing pit ready for the next jumper. When all is ready, the Number 6 Official will call the name of the next jumper. Number 6 Official may also help in checking for trailing leg fouls. Number 7 Official who is seated near the competitors' bench will relay the call for the next jumper.

When the Triple Jump event has been completed, the Head Triple Jump Official will give the completed event sheet to the Head Field Official.

Triple jump officials and the working crew will leave the field.

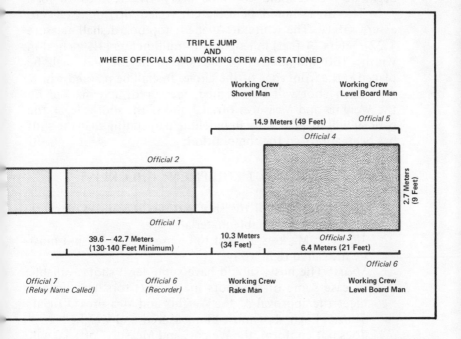

TRIPLE JUMP
AND
WHERE OFFICIALS AND WORKING CREW ARE STATIONED

Working Crew
Shovel Man

Working Crew
Level Board Man

14.9 Meters (49 Feet)   Official 5

Official 4

Official 2

2.7 Meters (9 Feet)

Official 1

39.6 – 42.7 Meters
(130-140 Feet Minimum)

10.3 Meters
(34 Feet)

Official 3
6.4 Meters (21 Feet)

Official 6

Official 7
(Relay Name Called)

Official 6
(Recorder)

Working Crew
Rake Man

Working Crew
Level Board Man

SHOT PUT

EQUIPMENT

1. Shots (for the appropriate level).
2. Scales.
3. Sideline Sector Metal Flags.
4. Measuring Tape—100-foot steel tape (English-metric).
5. Broom.
6. Chairs.
7. Name Indicator Boards.
8. Bench for the competitors.

The shot put circle is of concrete or some similar material. It is 2.135 meters in diameter (7 feet); the same diameter is used for all levels of competition.

Distance interval lines are optional and depend on the quality of the competition. At a top-rank collegiate meet they begin at 50 feet and continue every five feet to 70 feet.

The area should be isolated, roped off, or fenced to assure safety. The white arc-shaped stop-board shall measure 1.22 meters (4 feet) in length, 114 millimeters (4½ inches) in width, 100 millimeters (4 inches) in height and shall be placed at the front edge of the circle. It shall be painted white.

Each shot will be weighed, measured, and marked by the Weights and Measures official and if the shot is legal, the official will mark it with an indelible pen stating that the shot has been approved for competition.

THE SHOT PUT EQUIPMENT CHECKLIST

1. *The stop-board* of the shot put circle is made of wood or some other suitable material.
2. *Markers:* Markers are not to be used. Each fair put must be measured right away.
3. *Shots:* The hosts should have some legal shots available in case some of the shots the competitors have do not meet the approval of the Weights and Measures Official.
4. *Scales:* Each shot must be measured and weighed. If it does not conform, the Weights and Measures official will

impound the shot. If it meets the legal requirements, then the Weights and Measures official will mark it with a colored pen which will give the Shot Put official an indication that the shot has been approved for competition.

5. *Stop Watch:* One official will be responsible for keeping the allotted time the competitor has to complete his put (1½ min.).

6. *Foul/Fair Flags:* Number 1 Assistant Official should be responsible for these flags.

7. *Broom:* One of the assistant shot put officials should keep the shot put circle clean for each competitor.

8. *Chairs:* Officials Number 1, 2, and 3 should be seated when the competitor is ready to put.

9. *Metal Sector-Line Shot Put Flags:* These metal sector line flags are placed at each end of the sector lines.

10. *Name Indicator Boards:* These boards are used for the benefit of the spectators. They can inform the spectators who the next shot putter is, the round and the competitor's mark.

11. *Bench:* Shot put competitors who are not competing may be seated. This also gives the spectators a better view of the competition.

HEAD SHOT PUT OFFICIAL

1. Arrive at least 45 minutes before the shot put event is scheduled to begin and report to the Head Field official and also the Meet Director for instructions concerning the shot put.

2. Pick up the shot put recording sheets.

3. Check out the equipment and supplies to the assistant shot put officials.

4. Review the rules of the event with the assistant officials.

5. Assign the assistant officials to their areas.

6. Check the competitors in at least 15 minutes prior to the start of the event. Call each athlete's name and check them off on the recording sheet.

7. Notify competitors of the starting time and throwing order, and remind them again 5 minutes before the start.

8. Measurements are recorded to the lower ¼ inch or centimeter.
9. Inspect all shots and make sure all have been approved by the Weights and Measures official.
10. Line up the competitors for introductions, if needed.
11. At the end of the event, certify the results of the competition, and distribute the results as required.
12. Make sure all equipment is returned.

ASSISTANT SHOT PUT OFFICIALS

1. Arrive at least 30 minutes before the shot put is scheduled to begin and report to the Head Shot Put official.
2. Assist in keeping the shot put area clear of unauthorized personnel.
3. Indicate fair puts (white flag) and foul puts (red flag), if desired. Assist in marking and measuring puts.
4. Keep circle clean.

HELPFUL HINTS FOR SHOT PUT OFFICIALS

1. The shot must fall within the sector lines.
2. Competitors must leave the shot put circle from the rear half of the circle.
3. When the competitor takes his stance, the shot must be touching or close to the chin.
4. The shot shall not at any time drop behind the line of the shoulder during the put in the circle.
5. The competitor must not leave the circle until the shot hits the ground, and he/she must leave under control.
6. The shot must be a smooth solid sphere of iron or any other metal not softer than brass.
7. Each legal put should be measured immediately.
8. Shot put competitors may be allowed to compete in other events as long as they do not delay the shot put event. (This is true in all the other field events, as well.)
9. Taping two or more fingers together is not allowed.
10. Touching the top of the stop board, or any part of the area outside the circle while in the process of the put is a foul.
11. In case of a record, impound the implement immediately for weighing and measuring.

WHERE SHOT PUT OFFICIALS SHOULD BE STATIONED

Officials Number 1 (Head) and 2: They are seated outside the circle. One Official is on each side of the circle when the competitor is ready to put.

Official Number 2: He will be in charge of the measuring tape at the shot put circle.

Official Number 1: He will read and record the measurement.

Official Number 1 and 2 also watch for fouls in the circle and wave a white flag for fair puts, red for foul.

Official Number 3: It is his job to keep the rear area of the shot put cage clear of spectators. He is seated. He can also sweep the circle, as needed.

Officials Number 4 and 5: One Official is stationed on each side of the outside sector lines.

Officials Number 6 and 7: They spot where the shot falls (fair put) for measurement.

Official 6: He is also in charge of placing the rod of the measuring tape on the mark made by the shot.

The shot is never thrown or rolled back to the shot put circle. It is carried to the side of the sector line and returned to the athlete by hand. (It is recommended that a type of alley be set up so the shot can be returned to the competitors bench, such as the type used in bowling).

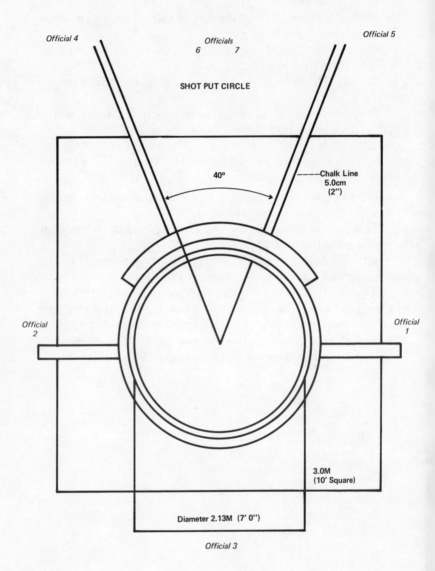

Official 4

Officials
6   7

Official 5

SHOT PUT CIRCLE

40°

Chalk Line
5.0cm
(2'')

Official
2

Official
1

3.0M
(10' Square)

Diameter 2.13M (7' 0'')

Official 3

DISCUS THROW

EQUIPMENT

1. *Markers (if needed).*
2. *Steel measuring tape (Meters and Feet).*
3. *Broom.*
4. *Chairs.*
5. *Stop watch.*
6. *Name Indicator Boards.*
7. *Bench for competitors.*

The discus circle (2.5 meters or 8 feet, 2½ in. inside diameter) is the same for High School, Colleges, Universities and other competition levels.

Side sector lines should be marked by tape or chalk. A metal flag shall be placed at each end of the sector lines.

The discus must land within the sector, which is a 40 degree radius from the throwing circle.

Each discus must be weighed and measured—if it conforms to regulations and specifications it will be marked with an indelible pen for approval by the Weights and Measures Official to be used in competition.

A "C" shaped cage is recommended for discus competition.

HEAD DISCUS OFFICIAL

1. Arrive at least one hour before the first scheduled discus event is to begin.
2. Obtain the list of competitors in the discus from the Head Field Official (or whoever has the list).
3. When the Assistant Discus Officials arrive, assign them to their positions and review their roles with them.
4. Check in the competitors and make sure all are present. Inform them of the order of throwing and the starting time.
5. Inspect each discus and be sure it has been approved by the Weights and Measures Official.
6. Line up competitors for introductions, if needed.

7. Keep the discus area free of spectators and other non-competitors.
8. Make sure each legal throw is measured immediately.
9. Certify the results of the competition and distribute the results, as required.
10. Make sure all equipment is returned to the appropriate place.

ASSISTANT DISCUS OFFICIALS

1. Arrive at least 45 minutes before the event is scheduled to begin.
2. Accept and carry out the assignment given to you by the Head Discus Official.
3. Mark and measure each throw immediately.
4. Check the recording sheets to make sure all the recordings are clear and easy to read.
5. Assist in keeping the discus area free of unauthorized personnel.
6. Keep the circle clean.
7. Indicate fair and foul throws (white and red flags).
8. Return all equipment to the Head Discus Official when the event is completed.

HELPFUL HINTS CONCERNING THE DISCUS

1. Competitors must not leave the circle on a legal throw until the discus hits the ground.
2. Competitors must leave the circle from the rear half of the circle, and under control.
3. It is illegal to use gloves when throwing the discus.
4. Competitors are permitted to use an adhesive substance in the circle or under their shoes.
5. The discus must be carried or conveyed back to the discus thrower or circle and is never to be thrown or rolled back.
6. In case of a record, impound the implement immediately for weighing and measuring.
7. Taping two or more fingers together is not allowed.

WHERE DISCUS OFFICIALS ARE POSITIONED

The numbers on the Discus Chart designate where each official is stationed and what his responsibility is in officiating the discus throw.

Officials Number 1 (Head) and 2 are seated when the competitor is ready to throw. One official is stationed on each side of the discus cage. The Number 2 Official is in charge of the measuring tape at the discus ring.

The Number 1 Official is responsible for reading and recording the measurement on the event card.

Number 1 and 2 also watch for fouls, waving the white or red flag, as appropriate.

Officials 3 and 4 are stationed on each side of the sector line to check out-of-sector throws. If the dicus goes out of the sector, the official on that side will wave his red flag indicating that the throw was a foul throw.

Officials 5, 6, and 7 mark the fair throws in the field.

Official Number 6 is in charge of the measuring tape in the field.

Official Number 8 is seated behind the discus cage to keep that area clear of spectators.

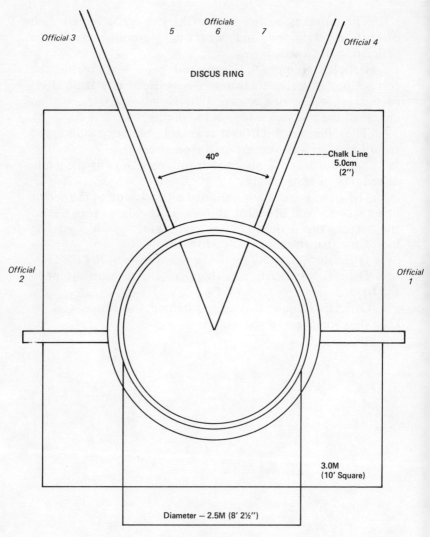

Official 3

Official 4

Officials
5   6   7

DISCUS RING

40°

--------Chalk Line
5.0cm
(2")

Official
2

Official
1

3.0M
(10' Square)

Diameter – 2.5M (8' 2½")

Official 8

-36-

HAMMER THROW

EQUIPMENT

1. *Steel Measuring Tape:* Meters and Feet (300') tapes.
2. *Broom:* The ring should be kept clean at all times during competition. This is a safety factor.
3. *Chairs:* Officials near the cage should be seated when the competitor is ready to throw. This gives the spectators a better view of the performance of each competitor.
4. *Name Indicator Boards:* It is important to post the name of the competitor and the round when the competitor is ready to throw, as spectators like to know who is in the ring. After the throw, post the mark achieved.
5. *Stop Watch:* One official will officially keep time so the competitor does not take more time than is allotted to complete the throw. It is a good idea if the school can afford to buy a big display (digital) timer to show competitors time remaining (1½ min. allotted).
6. *Bench for Competitors.*

HEAD HAMMER OFFICIAL

1. Arrive at least one hour before the hammer event is scheduled to begin.
2. Check each hammer for legality and safety and make sure they have been checked by the Weights and Measures Official.
3. Assign each Assistant Hammer Official to a position.
4. Obtain the list of competitors and recording sheets for the event from the Meet Director or Head Field official. Notify competitors of the throwing order.
5. Inform the Assistant Hammer Officials that the hammer must be carried back to the competitor.
6. Make sure the following items are on hand: broom, steel tape (300 feet), event recording sheet and a bench for the competitors to sit on when not competing.
7. Line up the competitors for introductions, if needed.

8. Certify the results of the competition and distribute results as required.
9. Make sure all equipment is returned to the proper place.

ASSISTANT HAMMER OFFICIALS

1. Arrive at least 30 minutes before the hammer event is scheduled to begin and report to the Head Hammer Official for assignment and instructions.
2. Carry out the assignment assigned to you by the Head Hammer Official to the best of your ability.
3. Mark and Measure each fair throw immediately.
4. Keep spectators a good distance away from the throwing and landing area.
5. Keep the circle clean.
6. Indicate fair and foul throws by waving white or red flag.

HELPFUL HINTS FOR HAMMER OFFICIALS

1. When the competitor is making his swings or turns, if the hammer touches the ground it is not a foul unless the competitor stops, interrupting the continuous movement.
2. If the hammer breaks during the throw or while in the air, it shall not be counted as a throw.
3. Gloves for the protection of the hands are permitted. The gloves must be smooth on the back and front and the fingertips must be exposed.
4. Taping 2 or more fingers together is not allowed, but use of tape on the wrist will be allowed (IAAF Rule 1980).
5. A belt of leather may be worn to protect the spine.
6. No type of substance may be sprayed or spread in the hammer circle.
7. Competitors must not leave the hammer circle until the hammer has hit the ground.
8. Competitors must leave the hammer circle from the back half of the hammer circle, and under control.
9. In case of a record, impound the implement immediately, for weighing and measuring.

WHERE HAMMER OFFICIALS ARE STATIONED

Number 1 (Head) and 2 Officials: Each official is stationed outside of the hammer circle cage. Both officials should have a red flag and a white flag.
Number 2 Official is responsible for the measuring tape in the circle.
Number 1 Official will read the measurement and record it.
Number 1 and 2 watch for fouls and indicate fair and foul throws by waving white or red flag.
Number 3 and 4 Officials: Each official will be stationed near the end of the sector lines to check out of bounds throws. They too should have red flags and white flags.
Number 5, 6, and 7 Officials: They will be stationed between the sector lines. All of them will check where the hammer lands. Wave red flag for out-of-sector throws.
Number 5 Official will also handle the measuring tape in the field.
Number 6 Official will place the rod where the hammer is marked. Number 5 and 7 find the marks.
Number 8 Official: He will keep the rear of the hammer circle clear of any disturbance. He will be seated.

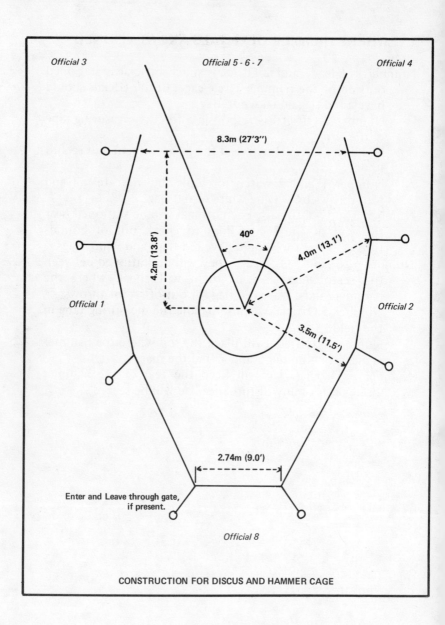

Official 3

Official 5 - 6 - 7

Official 4

8.3m (27'3")

4.2m (13.8')

40°

4.0m (13.1')

Official 1

Official 2

3.5m (11.5')

2.74m (9.0')

Enter and Leave through gate,
if present.

Official 8

CONSTRUCTION FOR DISCUS AND HAMMER CAGE

JAVELIN THROW

EQUIPMENT

1. *Measuring Tape:* A steel measuring tape (300 feet) is needed when measuring the javelin throw—feet/meters.
2. *Chairs:* Officials 1, 2, 8, and 9 should have chairs. They should be seated when the competitor is ready to throw.
3. *Sideline Sector Flags:* A metal flag is placed at each end of the sideline sector lines.
4. *Stop Watch:* One official should have a stop watch to time the competitor who should be informed that the time allotted to complete the throw is 1½ minutes.
5. *Broom:* It is important that a broom be placed near the javelin area just in case the javelin runway needs to be swept of any foreign matter.
6. *Javelin Rack:* It is advisable to have a javelin rack. When the javelins are not in use, they can be placed on the javelin rack. This is a safety factor.
7. *Bench For The Competitors:* Place a bench at least 10 feet away from the javelin runway. It is better to have the javelin competitors seated than roaming around.
8. *Name Indicator Board.*

The javelin shaft must be of metal or solid wood, have a cord grip and a metal point.

The runway or run-up is marked with two parallel lines which are 4 meters (13 feet, 1½ inches) apart. These terminate at the scratch arc line at the front of the runway.

HEAD JAVELIN OFFICIAL

The duties of the Head Javelin Official are here broken down into three parts:

1. *Duties before the competition:*
   A) Arrive at least 45 minutes before the event is scheduled to begin.
   B) Pick up the javelin event forms.
   C) Have the equipment needed delivered to the javelin area.

a) One 300 feet plastic tape and one steel tape (same length).
b) 5 red flags and 5 white flags, and two sector flags.
c) Rack-holder for the javelins.
D) Check javelin sector area for:
a) safety.
b) correct sector angle lines.
c) mark 8 meters (26 feet, 3 inches) behind the toe board on the javelin runway. This is the measuring point.
E) Assign the assistant javelin officials to their areas.
F) Make sure the Weights and Measures Official has checked and marked the javelins, as approved for competition.
G) Check in javelin competitors and inform them of the throwing order and how much time remains before the event is to begin.
H) Instruct the assistant javelin officials to check each javelin for any illegalities and also for any improper use of tape.
I) Instruct the assistant javelin officials concerning how and when to use the red flag and the white flag.
J) Appoint one assistant javelin official to display the marks of each competitor properly on the indicator board.
K) Line up javelin competitors for introductions, if needed.

2. *Duties during the competition:*
A) Inform the assistant javelin officials that the javelin event is to begin.
B) Have the competitors take their throws promptly (enforce the time rule—not to exceed 1½ minutes for each competitor).
C) Keep the event moving and do not let it drag.
D) Be sure that the athletes competing in the other events do not get too close to the javelin sector lines.
E) At the conclusion of the javelin preliminaries

certify which competitors have qualified for the finals and determine the order of competition.

3. *Duties after the competition has been concluded:*
   A) Certify the results of the competition.
   B) Distribute the results, as required.
   C) Appoint an assistant javelin official to escort the place winners to the awards stand, if needed.
   D) Make sure all javelin equipment is returned to the proper place.

ASSISTANT JAVELIN OFFICIALS

1. Arrive at least 45 minutes before the javelin is scheduled to begin.
2. Receive your assignment from the Head Javelin Official.
3. Check the javelins to verify they have been approved by the Weights and Measures Official.
4. Check for improper taping.
5. Station yourself so you do not hamper the view of the other javelin officials.
6. Assist in the tabulating of the results of the javelin throws.
7. Escort the place winners to the awards stand, if needed.

HELPFUL HINTS FOR JAVELIN OFFICIALS

1. The javelin must be thrown from behind the scratch arc line.
2. If the javelin breaks while in the air, it does not count as a throw, provided all other aspects of the throw were in accordance with the rules.
3. Use of tape on the hand is not allowed, except to cover a cut or wound.
4. Competitors may wear a belt for protection.
5. The javelin must be thrown with an over-the-shoulder motion; it cannot be slung or hurled.
6. To be recorded as a valid javelin throw, the tip of the metal head of the javelin must strike the ground before any other part of the javelin.
   NOTE: Meets governed by NCAA rules measure from whatever part of the javelin strikes first.

7. Competitors are not to leave the runway until the javelin has touched the ground.
8. In case of a record, impound the implement immediately for weighing and measuring.

WHERE JAVELIN OFFICIALS ARE STATIONED

The javelin "foul line" which is in the shape of an arc must be well placed, firm, and should be level with the runway. The arc shall be painted on a strip of wood or metal 70 millimeters (2¾ inches) in width. It must be painted white.

Officials should be stationed as shown on the javelin chart:

Officials Number 1 (Head) and 2 are seated on each side of the foul board line when the competitor is ready to throw. They watch for fouls and wave the white or red flag, as appropriate.

The Number 2 Official will be in charge of the measuring tape.

Number 1 Official will read the measurement and will record the reading on the event sheet.

Officials 3 and 4 will be stationed on each side of the sector lines. In case a throw goes outside of the sector lines, the official on whose side it goes out on will wave the red flag indicating that the throw was a foul throw.

Officials Number 5, 6, and 7 will be stationed behind the farthest measured line. They will mark where the fair javelin mark is made.

The Number 5 Official will be responsible for pinning the measuring tape in the field.

Number 6 and 7 Officials will mark the spot where the javelin made the mark and Number 5 Official will then place the rod of the measuring tape for measurement.

Officials Number 8 and 9 will keep the rear area of the runway clear of any spectators. This is a safety factor. The javelin is never thrown back, but is carried back to the javelin rack with the point toward the ground.

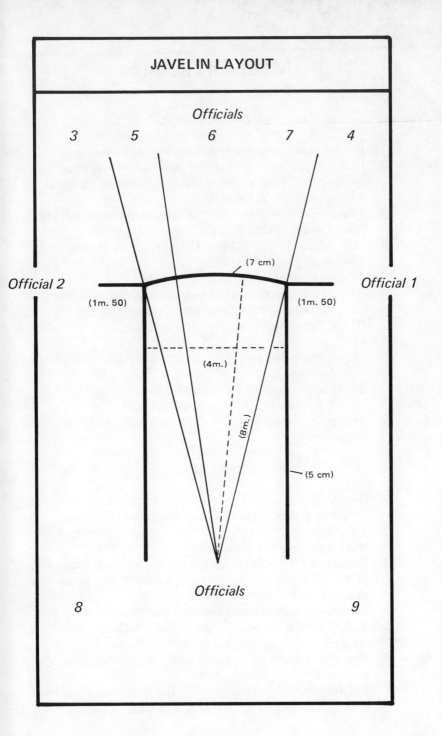

JAVELIN LAYOUT

Officials

3   5   6   7   4

Officials

(7 cm)

Official 2   Official 1

(1m. 50)   (1m. 50)

(4m.)

(8m.)

(5 cm)

Officials

8   9

MEET OFFICIALS

THE ANNOUNCER

1. He/she announces the results, scores and times.
2. It is recommended that the Announcer introduce the competitors, lane assignments, etc., prior to the event to enhance spectator interest.
3. The announcer gives calls for the events as indicated on the program or Call Sheet.
4. The Announcer can keep the spectators interested by announcing the following:
   A) New records.
   B) Past performances of outstanding competitors.
   C) Current league standings of teams.
   D) Leading runners.
   E) Lap times.
   F) Items of interest concerning the track meet or the runners.
   G) Field event distances and heights.
   H) Track rules or rulings when necessary.
5. The Announcer should talk slowly, distinctly, and be impartial.

REFEREE

1. Decide any questions which arise at the track meet for which no provision has been made in the rule book.
2. Emphasize to the officials that the rules governing the track meet will be carried out.
3. When the Finish Officials are unable to reach a decision as to who the winner is, the Referee will settle the placings.
4. Serve as an appeal agent for all protests.
5. Verify Interscholastic, State, City, National or World records.
6. Has the power to exclude competitors for improper conduct.
7. Recommend the changing of the location of a field event if conditions justify such a change.

8. Must be available to inform the press of any rulings which arise from violations and disqualifications.
9. Has the power to declare an event void and states when that event shall be held again.
10. Decide on protests or objections that involve the conduct of a competitor.

HEAD FIELD OFFICIAL

The position of the Head Field Official is one of immense responsibility, because the burden of making sure that the right decisions or rulings have been made is on him/her.

This Official must be able to render decisions with prudence and have good experience in field event officiating.

Rules are always subject to confirmation and approval of the Referee. The Head Field Official should be well-read and informed about all field event rules since he (or she) will be called upon from time to time to interpret them and render important decisions.

DUTIES OF THE HEAD FIELD OFFICIAL

1. Arrive at least one hour before the first field event is scheduled to begin.
2. Consult with the Meet Director regarding any variations of the rules for that area, etc.
3. Collect and have available all field event recording sheets.
4. Have a list of the officials who will be officiating the field events.
5. Meet with all the Head Officials of each field event before the field events are to begin. Clarify their duties concerning the number of trials, places, finals or any other necessary information for each event.
6. Check the sector lines to see that they are properly marked for the shot put, discus, javelin and hammer.
7. Check the diameter of the shot put, discus and hammer circles.
8. Inspect the standards of the pole vault and high jump.
9. Check the runways and take-off boards of the long and triple jump.

10. Assign or re-assign enough field officials to officiate each field event efficiently.
11. Assist when needed in measuring performances or implements, checking in the competitors to the various field events, etc.
12. Make sure all necessary equipment is at each field event area.
13. Supervise the measurement of a field event record performance.
14. Be available at all times to make decisions, especially in tie-breaking situations.
15. Check the results of each event card.
16. Instruct the Assistant Field Officials on the method of recording: successful, unsuccessful, or pass.
17. Be present until the final field event has been completed.
18. Assign a Field Event Official from each field event to escort the competitors from the checking area to the area of competition.
19. Make sure the field events start as scheduled.
20. Report any irregularities to the Referee for a final decision.
21. Instruct the assistant officials that measurements shall be the lesser quarter-inch or centimeter in the field events except in the case of the discus, javelin and hammer which will be recorded to the lesser whole inch.
22. Instruct the assistant officials that all measurements in each field event must be read by two officials.
23. Remind the assistant officials to enforce the rules governing that event and to prevent any unnecessary delays in the competition.
24. Do not allow any further practice after the conclusion of any field event.
25. Make any recommendations or suggestions concerning the improvement of the field events and give to the Meet Director.

HEAD FINISH JUDGE

1. Arrive at least one hour before the first scheduled running event.
2. Be responsible for the assigning of the Assistant Finish

Officials to their "place-pickings."

3. Make sure the entire finish is viewable by the judges in order to prevent individual runners from being overlooked.
4. Record finishes as reported by the Assistant Finish Officials.
5. Make sure that the place winners and times of the competitors are recorded (legibly) on the event recording sheets.
6. Record finish and/or times from the Photo-Timer Official (if used) as soon as possible.
7. Make decisions if the Assistant Finish Officials cannot agree on a certain placing.
8. Assign at least two Assistant Finish Officials to each "place-picking" and place each one on opposite sides of the finish line, if possible.
9. Note—decisions of the Assistant Finish Officials shall be final and without appeal except for possible action taken by the Head Finish Official, Referee, or the Jury of Appeal.
10. Examine the photo-timing picture with the Head Photo-Timing Official of each finish.
11. Notify the Starter that all Assistant Finish Officials are "ready" by waving a white flag and "not ready", by waving the red flag for each event. (This function can be assigned to an assistant finish official.)

ASSISTANT FINISH JUDGES

1. Arrive at least thirty minutes before the first scheduled running event is to take place.
2. Report to the Head Finish Official for assignment.
3. Follow the runners after finishing the race and get the runners' names and team affiliations and report to the Head Finish Official with the places picked for the runners.
4. Do not try to tell the other Assistant Finish Officials how to pick places.
5. Base your decision on the torso (not the arms, legs or head).
6. Remember the number, color of the uniform and the lane assigned to the runner.

7. Do not discuss the place-picking with the other officials.
8. An Assistant Finish Official picking for the higher place has precedence over the Official picking for the lower place.
9. Always consult the Head Finish Official in case of any problems.
10. Do not socialize—do your own job.

HEAD TIMING OFFICIAL

1. Arrive at least forty-five minutes before the first event is scheduled to begin and review the rules for the meet with the Meet Director.
2. Assemble the Assistant Timers and go over the basic rules with them.
3. Assign each Assistant Timer to a place according to evaluation. Also check each Timer's watch.
4. Be alert to the order of finish of each race (if 4th place Timer is faster than 3rd place Timer, for instance).
5. Read and record each Timer's watch immediately after each race.
6. Select the winning time for first place on the basis of the two agreeing watches or the middle watch.
7. Assign one Assistant Timer to call out lap-times.
8. When a record is being considered, check each watch, and also have the Referee check the watches.
9. Acquaint yourself with the record of each race.
10. Procure enough Recording Event Sheets.
11. Give undivided attention to your duties and instruct the Assistant Timers to do likewise.
12. Always make sure the Assistant Timers are ready before the Starter is signaled.
13. All hand-timed races on the track are recorded to the 1/10th second. Events which are held partly or entirely outside the stadium (e.g., walks, marathon, etc.) will be converted to the next longer full second, even if a photo-timer is used. 2:10:44.4, for instance, should be recorded as 2:10:45. Where a fully automatic photo-timer is used, races up to 10,000m are recorded to the 1/100th second. Longer races on the track are converted to the next 1/10th second.
14. Keep the area clear of unauthorized persons.

15. Assign Assistant Timers to places:
    a) Three Assistant Timers for first place (and an alternate).
    b) Two Assistant Timers to each of the remaining places.

FINISH-YARN HOLDERS

16. Recent thought is to not use yarn at the finish line, as too many Finish Officials watch the yarn and not the finish line on the track. Also, the yarn has burned and cut many athletes.
17. *If Finish-Yarn is used:*
    Keep the finish-yarn tight so it will break on contact. Do not release the yarn, because this is what burns and cuts athletes. Instruct the Finish-Tape Holders when to stretch the yarn across the finish line.

ASSISTANT TIMING OFFICIALS

1. Arrive at least thirty minutes before the first running event and report to the Head Timer.
2. Follow instructions given to you by the Head Timer.
3. Always be ready when the race is to start.
4. Make sure your stop watch is in good working order.
5. Do not anticipate the finish.
6. Do own timing and not someone else's.
7. Watch runner and stop watch when the runner's torso hits the finish line.
8. Show watch to the Head Timer after each race and do not clear it until the Head Timer so instructs.
9. Never yell time down to the finish line.

HEAD INSPECTOR

1. Arrive at least thirty minutes before the meet is scheduled to begin.
2. Consult with the Referee and the Meet Director.
3. Assign the Assistant Inspectors to their areas.
4. Supervise and assist the Assistant Inspectors should there be a close judgment call.
5. In the hurdle events, check the hurdles for proper

spacing and also see if the hurdles are adjusted correctly.

6. Report violations from the Assistant Inspectors to the Referee.
7. When the Inspectors are not inspecting, they can assist the Marshals.
8. Make sure each Assistant Inspector has the necessary equipment and supplies to carry out the duties of Inspector.

ASSISTANT INSPECTORS

1. Arrive at least fifteen minutes before the first scheduled running event and report to the Head Inspector for your assignment.
2. In case of a violation, wave your red flag. Write what the violation is on the violation card and give it to the Head Inspector. Keep a copy for your records.
3. Do not discuss the violation with anyone but the Head Inspector.
4. Wave the white flag indicating that you are ready and that the track is clear.
5. Observe the runners during the race for any illegal crowding, jostling, cutting-in, lane violations, etc.
6. Assist the Marshals when not inspecting.

WHERE INSPECTORS SHOULD BE STATIONED

Inspectors may be stationed on the outer edge of the track or the inner edge of the track. They should not get on the track until all the runners have passed.

If the field events are in progress, then the best place to be stationed would be the outer edge of the track.

Eight Inspectors can do an adequate job of inspecting, but a few more would be helpful.

Number 1 Inspector	is generally the Head Inspector and he stations himself at the first turn so all the Assistant Inspectors will know where he is at all times.
Number 2 Inspector	will be stationed at turn two(2).
Number 3 Inspector	will be stationed at turn three (3).
Number 4 Inspector	will be stationed at turn four (4).

Number 5 Inspector	will be stationed at the backstretch.
Number 6 Inspector	will be stationed at the homestretch.
Number 7 Inspector	will be stationed between Number 1 and Number 2 Inspectors.
Number 8 Inspector	will be stationed between Number 3 and Number 4 Inspectors.

HEAD MARSHAL

1. Arrive at least one hour before any of the scheduled events are to begin.
2. Report to the Referee and the Meet Director and go over the rules of marshaling with them.
3. Take charge of the area where the track meet is to take place.
4. Allow only active competitors, officials and authorized personnel in the area.
5. Assist the Timers and Finish Officials by keeping the photographers and unauthorized persons clear of the finish line.
6. Assign each Assistant Marshal to an area.
7. Make sure each Assistant Marshal understands the duties of marshaling.
8. In case of out-of-hand violent action call for police assistance.

ASSISTANT MARSHALS

1. Report to the Head Marshal at least thirty minutes before the meet is scheduled to begin.
2. Carry out your assignment as assigned to you by the Head Marshal.
3. Remember to be polite, but firm, when asking a person to leave the area.
4. If you have any problems consult with the Head Marshal.

HEAD PHOTO-TIMER OFFICIAL

1. Assemble the photo-timing machine and make sure it is in good working order.

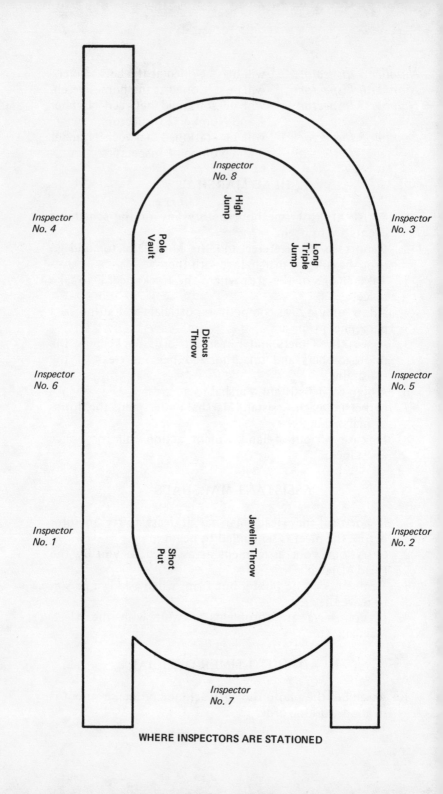

WHERE INSPECTORS ARE STATIONED

2. Work closely with the Head Timer and the Head Finish Official.
3. Review the photograph with the Assistant Photo-Timing Officials.
4. After viewing the photograph and determining the places, report the findings of your committee to the Head Finish Official.
5. In case you and the Assistant Photo-Timing Officials have a problem determining the order of finish, consult the Head Finish Official. The Referee may also be consulted.
6. Photo-Timing Officials shall consist of three persons and only they are permitted to be on the platform of the photo-timing machine.
7. It is recommended that the photo-timing picture not be passed around to other persons.
8. Make sure the Starter understands your signals.
9. File the photographs in a sturdy box when the track meet has concluded.
10. Make sure that all the equipment is well-packed and return it to the proper area.
11. Check with the Referee, Meet Director, Head Timer and the Head Finish Official for any last minute adjustments or instructions.

ASSISTANT PHOTO-TIMING OFFICIALS

1. Arrive at least one hour before the first track meet is scheduled to begin to assist the Head Photo-Timing Official.
2. Carry out your assignment without any hesitation.
3. Check the photo-film box for sufficient film.
4. Keep unauthorized persons (such as the Timers and Finish Officials) away from the photo-timing platform.
5. Do not call out who the place winners are.

JURY OF APPEAL

In large meets or championships, a Jury of Appeal is normally designated to deal with protests. This group should consist of at least three, not more than five, experienced officials (who may have other officiating duties at the meet;

the Referee and Head Field Official are often members of the Jury of Appeal).

Protests should first be made orally to the Referee by the athlete or coach (or other authorized person). The Referee may render a decision or refer the matter to the Jury. If not satisfied with the Referee's decision, an appeal may be made to the Jury directly. This appeal must be in writing. The Jury must consider all available evidence and interview those considered necessary to arrive at a fair decision.

THE STARTER

1. Arrive at least one hour before the start of the first event and report to the Meet Director.
2. Check where the starts and finishes are located. Check staggers for each race.
3. Check mechanism of gun and supply of shells. Use a .32 (minimum) caliber blank pistol.
4. Make sure the Timers, Finish Judges and Photo-Timing Officials are ready before you start the event.
5. Take control of the competitors at the starting-line.
6. Use a microphone or other amplification device (if the competitors can not hear you because of noise).
7. Place yourself equidistant from all competitors.
8. Observe the competitors after the start and until the race has finished.
9. Never allow spectators to interrupt the smooth starting of a race.
10. Meet with the inspectors and make sure they understand where the relay passing zones are.

THE ASSISTANT (RECALL) STARTER

1. Arrive at least one hour before the first running event is to begin and report to the Head Starter.
2. Review the rules for the track meet, familiarizing yourself with the starts, staggers and the finishes of each event.
3. Assist in controlling the competitors at the starting-line.
4. Make sure the pistol is in good working order and that you have enough shells, a rule book and whistle.

5. Position self to have a clear and complete view of the start.
6. When a recall is ordered, assemble the competitors immediately. Recall by firing your pistol.
7. Assist the Starter as needed.
8. Help keep the track meet on schedule.

CHIEF WALK OFFICIAL

1. Arrive at least one hour before the first walking event is scheduled to begin and acquaint yourself with the course the walkers will use.
2. Meet with the Assistant Walk Officials and brief them on the walking rules.
3. Assign the Assistant Walk Officials to their posts.
4. Position officials so they can make decisions clearly and uninterruptedly.
5. Stress to the Assistant Walking Officials that they must maintain dignity, independence and ensure impartiality throughout the walking race.
6. Have violation cards with you during the race.

ASSISTANT WALKING OFFICIALS

1. Arrive at least thirty minutes before the walking event is scheduled to begin and report to the Chief Walk Official.
2. Check the course the walkers will use for the race.
3. Carry out instructions given to you by the Chief Walk Official.
4. Get a program listing the walkers.
5. Do not take your attention from your duties when officiating.
6. Observe each walker and always record an infraction when you call it.
7. Do not converse with the other officials or the walkers during competition.
8. Remember, it is the duty of the Chief Walk Official to disqualify and notify a walker when such a decision is called for.
9. Do not caution a walker unless you are sure.
10. Never coach a walker during competition.

WALKIE-TALKIE CREW

1. Circulate among the field event areas and report the marks in each of the field events to the Announcer.
2. Ascertain the names of the leaders and their best efforts.
3. Keep the Announcer aware of any noteworthy performances.
4. Do not interfere with the officiating officials, or competing athletes.
5. Take special care in the throwing events areas.
6. When the track meet has concluded, return your walkie-talkie to the proper place.

SCOREKEEPING

1. Record accurately all the results the officials have recorded on the event cards into the scorebook.
2. Determine the score at any given time:
   (A) *Dual Track Meets*
       5 points for first place
       3 points for second place
       1 point for third place
       Relays: 5 points for first, no points for second.
   (B) *Triangular Meets*
       5 points for first place
       3 points for second place
       2 points for third place
       1 point for fourth place
       Relays: 5 points for first, 3 points for second, no points for third place.

HEAD CLERK OF THE COURSE

1. Arrive at least one hour before the first scheduled track event is to begin.
2. Pick up the track event sheets from the Meet Director.
3. Meet with the Head Finish Official and have him check the entries on the recording event sheets for each event with you.
4. Make sure each Assistant Clerk of the Course has a rule book for the meet and the necessary items needed for clerking.

5. Assign the Assistant Clerks of the Course to duties that will be helpful in keeping the track meet on schedule.
6. Be responsible for recording the names and numbers of competitors entered in each event.
7. Assign each competitor to the proper heat and the proper lane.
8. Instruct the competitors in the rules that govern that event.
9. Hold each competitor responsible for reporting to the starting line promptly. Make sure all have numbers, if provided by meet director.
10. Make sure the athletes are collected and conducted to the starting line before each race.
11. Make adjustments in the heats or lane assignments if necessary.
12. Provide the Head Finish Official with the event recording sheet for the race.
13. Keep the competitors informed as to the time of their assigned event.
14. After the meet has concluded, be sure no loose ends are undone. Settle any complaints before leaving the track site.

ASSISTANT CLERKS OF THE COURSE

1. Arrive at least thirty minutes before the first scheduled event is to begin and report to the Head Clerk of the Course.
2. Carry out the duties assigned to you by the Head Clerk of the Course.
3. Assist the Head Clerk of the Course in keeping the track meet on schedule.
4. Do not socialize when on duty.
5. Avoid taking part in any unnecessary remarks from the spectators.

LAP COORDINATOR

The Head Finish Official shall appoint an official to operate the lap counter. This official keeps track of the number of laps remaining in races over a mile and, using his lap counter, indicates the laps remaining as each runner passes the finish line point. It is a good idea for this official to have an assistant who times the leader each lap, providing the lap coordinator with important back-up information on laps run and laps to go.

HEAD WIND GAUGE OPERATOR

1. Arrive at least 30 minutes before the first event and set up the wind gauge machines.
2. Determine the starting times of each event to be monitored by the wind gauge. Obtain wind readings for the following durations:
    a) Long Jump, Triple Jump ... 5 seconds
    b) 100 Meter Run, 200 Meter Run .. 10 seconds
    c) 100 or 110 Meter Hurdles ... 13 seconds
3. Complete wind-reading cards for each jump and run.
4. Records will not be sanctioned if the wind-reading is over 2 meters per second.
5. Assign Assistant Wind Gauge Operators
    a) to read the wind gauge.
    b) to record their readings.
    c) to report the readings to the appropriate official.
6. Supervise the Assistant Wind Gauge Operators.
7. Retain wind-gauge readings of each event.
8. Secure and return the wind gauges to the proper place after the track meet and make sure the wind readings have been recorded correctly before leaving the area.

ELECTRONIC WIND GAUGE OPERATION

Instructions on how to operate the wind gauge will be enclosed when the machine is delivered, but the following will be helpful:
Where to place and how to operate an electronic wind gauge machine:
The 100-Meter Dash:
Place the wind gauge halfway down the track and not more than two meters away from the track. Set the wind velocity gauge at the ten second mark. When you see the flash or the smoke from the Starter's gun, press the electronic switch on the wind gauge and the machine will record the wind velocity reading and give you a print out.

The 110- and 100-Meter Hurdles:
Use the same procedure as was used for the 100 meter dash except the wind gauge is set at the 13-second mark.
The 200-Meter Dash:
The wind gauge is placed halfway between the finishline and the curve and not more than two meters from the straightaway.
The gauge is set at the 10-second mark.
The Long and Triple Jumps:
The wind gauge is placed not more than two meters from the runway and at least 40 meters from the take-off board for the long-jump and 35 meters for the triple-jump.
The wind gauge is set at the 5-second mark for the long jump and the triple jump.
When the competitor begins his run (for the long jump and the triple jump), press the electronic switch for the wind velocity reading.

EVENT RECORDING SHEETS (See p. 62)

Instructions To The Officials:

1. Consult with the Meet Referee or the Head Field Official when you are confronted with any problems concerning the competition.
2. When the event has been concluded, record the competitors' final placings in the proper column, usually at the bottom of page (not shown).
3. In case of a record, be sure the proper steps are taken to insure that the implements and/or the competing area conform to legal status. Meet Referee should be alerted immediately.
4. Upon completion of the event, please *sign* the recording sheets and return them to the Scorer's table immediately.

These Track Event Recording Forms can be purchased from:

The Athletics Congress/U.S.A.
P.O. Box 120
Indianapolis, Indiana 46206

FIELD EVENT RECORDING SHEET

LONG JUMP - TRIPLE JUMP - SHOT PUT

DISCUS - HAMMER - JAVELIN

EVENT NO.

TOTAL ENTRIES

FLIGHTS

NO. OF PLACES

MEET

DATE

PLACE

MEET RECORD

COMPETITOR	NO.	AFFILIATION	MEASURED DISTANCE																	BEST DISTANCE		METRIC DISTANCE
			TRIALS						FINALS													
			1		2		3		1		2		3							ft.	in.	
			ft	in.	ft	in.	ft	in.	ft	in.	ft	in.	ft	in.								

-62-

MEET PREPARATION

CHECK LIST FOR TRACK MEET PREPARATION
DIRT TRACKS

Meet: _____

VS _____ _____

Date:_____ Time: _____

Starting Time of Field Events:_____

Starting Time of Track Events: _____

1. *Day before the Track Meet:*
    A) Water the track.
    B) Check landing pits.
        a) High Jump.
        b) Pole Vault.
    C) Have infield lawn mowed.
    D) Loosen and level sand in the long and triple jump
        pits. (Water lightly.)
    E) Lock the gates to the track area when finished.
2. *Day of the Track Meet:*
    A) Drag the track.
    B) Sprinkle the track lightly.
    C) Mark entire track with chalk-line lanes.
    D) Mark Starts and Finishes.
        a) Finish line--In white.
        b) Starts--In white.
        c) Staggers—In blue (broken-lines).
        d) Relay Zones—In red.
    E) Check long and triple jump boards.
    F) Set up flights of hurdles.
    G) Smooth and level high jump area.
    H) Set up high jump and pole vault standards.
    I) Place crossbars at pole vault and high jump areas.
    J) Rake, smooth, roll and sprinkle runways.

a) Long Jump.
b) Pole Vault.
c) High Jump.
d) Triple Jump.
e) Javelin.

K) Stepladder (4.6 Meters should be available) at pole vault area.
L) Bar replacer at the pole vault pit.
M) Broom at each field event area:
a) Discus.
b) High jump.
c) Long and triple jump.
d) Pole vault.
e) Shot put.
f) Javelin.
g) Hammer.

N) Keep the field event areas clean.
O) Mark sectors and distance lines in the throwing events with chalk lines.
P) Set up benches for the bull-pens.
Q) Lock all the gates to the track except the entrance gates to the bleachers.
R) Set up starting blocks for the first race.
S) Rope off straightaway from the stands.
T) Chairs and tables for the Official Scorers, Clerk and Announcer. Chairs for field event officials. Judges stand.

3. *Conclusion of the Meet:*
A) Make sure the Head Manager has checked in all equipment and supplies.
B) Give the track and field areas a final check before you leave.

CHECK LIST FOR TRACK MEET PREPARATION—
ALL WEATHER TRACKS

Meet: _____

_____ VS _____

Date: _____ Time: _____

Starting Time for the Field Events: _____

Starting Time for the Track Events: _____

1. *Day before the Track Meet:*
    A) Sweep the track and the field event runways and the rings.
    B) Have the gardener mow the lawn in the infield.
    C) Mark "distance lines" in the field events and place sector flags.
    D) Place benches at each field event area.
    E) Check long and triple jump boards.
    F) Water, level and smooth the long and triple jump sand pits.
    G) Lock all the gates when you have finished.
2. *The day of the Track Meet:*
    A) Set up the flights of hurdles for the first race.
    B) Place high jump and pole vault standards.
    C) Have crossbars at the high jump and the pole vault areas.
    D) Have a pole vault crossbar replacer at the pole vault pit.
    E) Check and secure the pole vault and high jump landing pits.
    F) Sweep runways if needed.
    G) Set up starting blocks for the first race.
    H) Place the Scorer's table in an area away from any interference.
    I) Have a 15-foot ladder available at pole vault area.
    J) Arrange to have a broom at each field event area.
    K) Be certain that each field event area has the necessary equipment: chairs, flags, shovels, etc.
    L) Judges stand.

3. *Conclusion of the Track Meet:*
   A) Make sure the Head Manager has checked in all the track equipment and supplies.
   B) Give the track and field areas a final check before you leave.

ORGANIZING THE MEET

1. *Preparing The Facilities:*
   A) Do as much work as possible in preparing the track the day before a track meet. This will mean less work the day of the meet and will allow you to take care of other minor needs.
   B) Obtain as much help as possible:
      1. Meet with the Supervising Custodian and the Head Gardner to obtain assistance from their departments.
      2. Organize student assistance.
      3. Use motorized vehicle for moving equipment.
2. *Officials:*
   A) Meet Manager—Select a reliable person who is knowledgeable in putting on track and field meets.
   B) Obtaining Officials:
      1. Organize a Track and Field Officials Association.
      2. Assign members of the Faculty or Parents.
      3. Use student volunteers or student clubs.
      4. Contact community organizations.
      5. If funds are available, pay for the help.
   C) Instructing Officials:
      1. Have a meeting with the Field Event Officials and go over the important areas of each event.
      2. Also have a meeting with the rest of the officials.
      3. Make sure the officials are familiar with the rule book governing the meet.
      4. Give the officials helpful hints and aids for officiating. Check lists in the front of this book will be of great help.
      5. Use experienced help to assist you when you are instructing the group.
      6. Have officials get experience during time trials, and practices.
      7. Paste the rules on the back of clipboards for the particular events.
      8. Hand out printed information to the officials

regarding the schedule of events for track meets.

D) Assigning Officials:

1. Make sure you have enough officials assigned to each area.

2. Assign officials according to their interests.

3. The Clerk of the Course is considered one of the most important officials. Select a person who can keep the track meet on the time schedule.

   a) The Clerk of the Course should be a person who is knowledgeable about track meets.

   b) The Clerk of the Course should have at least one other person assisting him.

   c) He should take charge of the athletes competing in upcoming running events.

4. Rotating Officials:

   If there is a shortage of officials for the track meet, the following suggestions may be helpful:

   a) Start the field events at least forty-five minutes before the first running event is scheduled to begin. As these events are completed, those Officials can assist in the other events.

   b) The use of the Chronomix or other multi-timer is very useful in timing distance runs and also, some flat races. This machine can replace many hand timers. (The Chronomix can be purchased from Chronomix Corporation, 650F Vaqueros Avenue, Sunnyvale, California 94086)

   c) The Photo-Timer will also replace many Timers and Finish Officials. This machine will not only take the picture of the finish of the race, but will also record the time of each runner. However, some hand timers will be needed in the event of photo-timer failure.

d) Assign students to assist faculty members.

e) Combine some of the assignments; such as: the Starter can be the Clerk and Referee as well.

    The Scorer can also assist at the finish line, as a judge or timer.

    Many of the Field Event Officials can assist at the finish line by picking places and timing.

    Timers can time two runners by using split timing watches.

    The use of "split timing watches" is very useful. The 12-timing watch can time 12 runners. It can be purchased from: International Dictating Equipment, Airport International Plaza, 125 Wilbur Place, Bohemia, New York 11716.

f) Athletes from other sports can help.

5. Announcer should be familiar with Track and Field Meets:

a) He/She should have a time schedule of events of the Track Meet.

b) The Announcer should have at least three assistants.

c) The public address system should be in good working order.

d) Announce the results as soon as they are received from the Head Finish Official and the Head Field Official.

e) The Announcer is in a good position to control the crowd and keep it interested by giving them interesting facts concerning the meet.

f) He/She should never make announcements after the Starter has alerted the Finishline Officials that the race is to begin.

6. The Hurdle Captain should know his job and crew:

a) Preferably, this should be the Hurdle Captain's sole responsibility.

b) Each member of the Hurdle Crew should be identified by wearing a special shirt or a ribbon.

c) Assign two members of the Hurdle Crew to be responsible for each flight of hurdles.

7. Starting Block Assistants:

a) Each Starting Block Attendant should have a mallet (for dirt tracks) and a wing-nut wrench.

b) One Attendant is responsible for the wheelbarrow or the Starting Block Carrier.

c) Starting Block Crew should preferably have no other duties.

d) Attendants should be experienced in adjusting blocks.

e) One Attendant is responsible for two starting blocks.

f) The person who has had experience working with starting blocks at previous track meets should supervise.

8. Scorekeeper:

a) The person taking care of the scoring should know the scoring procedure thoroughly.

b) Assign the same person for the entire track season.

c) Explain and instruct how-to-score a track meet during trials, practice meets and meetings.

9. Inspectors:

a) Assign personnel who like to be Inspectors and are willing to study the rules and are not shy about calling violations.

b) An Inspector should have a red flag (waved in case of a violation) and a white flag (waved when all is fair; it also informs the Starter that he is ready).

c) Inspectors should watch for jostling, or cutting-in. They will also watch for lane violations (for races run in lanes), cutting in too early, baton passing out of zone, etc. All violations should be reported to the Referee right away.

    d)   Demonstrations and pictures are very helpful aids when instructing Inspectors.

10. Head Field Official:

    a)   This person should be well-experienced in track and field (especially in the field events).

    b)   Circulates to each field event.

    c)   Makes decisions concerning violations.

    d)   It is the duty of the Head Field Official to see that the field events start as scheduled.

    e)   Settles disputes and enforces the rules.

    f)   Schedules a meeting prior to the meet and reviews the rules with the Field Officials.

    g)   Assigns officials during practice and time trials so they can gain experience.

    h)   Keeps a record of what has to be done that would improve the field events.

    i)   Establishes a method of procedures for the officials to follow.

    j)   Makes sure that each field event official has received a program of the track meet.

    k)   The Head Field Official is responsible for checking the measuring tapes and the equipment.

    l)   Consults with each Head Field Event Official before they leave the area in regards to any improvements in conducting the field events.

11. Place-Pickers (Finish Judges):

    a)   If experienced Officials are not available, the faculty or students can help for a dual track meet.

    b)   Schedule a meeting to brief Place-Pickers for the meet.

    c)   Place-Pickers should be identified by uniform, special shirt or ribbon.

d) Stress the selecting of a Messenger to deliver the completed results of each event to the correct individuals:
   1. Announcer.
   2. Scorer.
   3. Recorder.
e) Assign two Place-Pickers to each place.

12. Timers:
   a) If experienced officials are not available, assign coaches, faculty members or qualified students to be Timers.
   b) Instruct the officials how to use a stopwatch.
   c) The Head Timer is in charge of the watches and will read each watch after each of the events.

13. General Assistance:
   a) Have a student meet the visiting track team and escort them to where they are to assemble.
   b) The Head Manager or one of the Assistant Managers should go over the starting areas, finishes, Clerk of the Course location and the general conduct of the meet for the visiting school's Head Manager or Coach.
   c) Ideally, an information brochure should be given to each member of the visiting track team.
      1. A map of the starts and finishes.
      2. Records of the school and stadium.
      3. Time schedule of the track and field events.
   d) Assign faculty members and students to act as marshals in keeping the infield clear of anyone who is not participating in the track meet.
   e) If necessary, the athletic teams of other sports can be of great assistance.

3. *Equipment*
   A) Field event equipment should be placed at each area before the visiting team arrives.
   B) Physical Education classes can be of great help in

setting up field equipment.

C) Make sure there is a rake, two shovels (one pointed and one square nosed), and a leveling board at the long jump and triple jump pits.

D) Have a bar-replacer at the pole vault pit.

E) Set up a Scorekeeper's area with a table and chairs.

F) Set the hurdles prior to track meet and also rope-off the Finish and Timing Officials' Areas.

G) Place the elevated stands for the Place-Pickers and the Timers.

TRACK MANAGERS' DUTIES

1. *Head Manager:*
   A) Must be responsible for carrying out all duties requested by the Head Track Coach.
   B) Is responsible for all track equipment.
   C) Should organize an Assistant Managers' Crew and instruct them in their responsibilities.
   D) Have the necessary equipment out for each day, and know where it is to be placed.
   E) Should make sure that the equipment is taken in at the conclusion of the daily track work-out and put in proper place.
   F) Issue uniforms and keep an accurate record of each item.
   G) Mark all track equipment for identifying purposes.
   H) Notify the Head Track Coach if any equipment is in need of repair or replacing.
   I) Keep the equipment room neat, clean and orderly at all times.
   J) Record each performance accurately of each track athlete during meets and practices.
   K) Appoint an Assistant Manager to keep the track bulletin board up-to-date and accurate.
   L) Check to ensure that the proper equipment is available for the home track meets. See Equipment Check List on page 78.
   M) Alert the Head Track Coach of any items that may have been overlooked or are missing.
   N) Assist the track athletes prior to the Track Meet.
   O) Establish an area as the "Nerve Center" where all equipment operations will take place.
2. *Timing Managers (Assistants):*
   A) Time the runners who would like to be timed during the workouts.
   B) Record and keep accurate results of the timed workouts.
   C) Keep accurate times of the runners in the meet.
   D) Clean and clear the towel room at the end of the workouts and the track meets.

E)   Take care of the stopwatches and do not allow any-
     one to use them without consent of the Head Manager.
F)   Keep a record to whom you issued the measuring tapes.

3. *Uniform Managers (Assistants):*
A)   Make sure no uniform parts are left at the meet or
     the workouts.
B)   Be responsible for the sweat suits by taking them
     from the starting line to the bull-pen during a meet.
C)   Issue the track uniforms to the athletes for the
     meet and keep an accurate record to whom each
     item was issued.
D)   Keep the uniform room neat, clean and orderly at
     all times.
E)   Assist the Timing Managers when needed.

4. *Equipment Manager (Assistants):*
A)   Keep all the track equipment clean and in good
     condition.
B)   Issue and record all issues of equipment.
C)   Keep equipment room neat, clean and orderly.
D)   Mark all track equipment.
E)   Take charge of the equipment at away track meets.
F)   Check out   vaulting poles, crossbars, starting
     blocks, rakes and other equipment necessary for
     the workout sessions.
G)   Assist whenever needed during workouts or meets.
H)   Run errands or assist the Head Manager if he needs
     assistance.
I)   Keep the towel and locker rooms neat, clean and
     orderly before and after the visiting team leaves.
J)   Sweep the runways if they need attention.
K)   Paint the long and triple jump boards if they need
     painting.
L)   Keep the inside lane of the track free from dirt
     build-up.
M)   Keep an accurate check on the conditions of the
     runways, sand pits and landing mats.
N)   Stack the hurdles at the conclusion of each work-
     out and at the same time check each hurdle for any
     sort of damages.
O)   Assist in other departments if one of the Assistant
     Managers is absent during the workouts or the day
     of a track meet.

HEAD HURDLE MANAGER

1. Keep Hurdle Crew together.
2. Use a wagon to move hurdles to the areas (400-meter race).
3. Know when and where to move the hurdles.
4. Assign attendants to flights of hurdles.
5. After the hurdle race, have the Hurdle Crew remove the hurdles from the track and adjust them for the next hurdle event.
6. When each hurdle has been placed properly for the race, check each flight for alignment and correct height.
7. At the conclusion of the meet, have the Hurdle Crew take the hurdles to the storage shack and stack them properly.
8. Make sure each hurdle is in good condition before stacking.

HURDLE CREW

1. Report to the Head Hurdle Manager at least 45 minutes before the first race.
2. Carry out instructions given to you by the Head Hurdle Manager.
3. Make sure each hurdle in your flight is at the right height.

CHECK LIST

A) Coach:
   1. *Check eligibility of each athlete.*
   2. *Post the schedule of events for the track meet.*
   3. *Get event cards ready. Check if they are properly filled out.*
   4. *Submit entries in each event.*
   5. *Post the names of the athletes who will be competing in the track meet.*
   6. *Check the condition of the track and the field.*
   7. *Make sure a Doctor is assigned.*
   8. *Send the newspapers any publicity about the track meet.*
   9. *Allot tickets for the meet.*

B) Managers:
1. *Organize a hurdle crew.*
2. *Make sure the visitors' room is clean, neat and orderly.*
3. *Check equipment (for home meets).*
4. *Have an adequate supply of items that will be needed for the track meet.*

EQUIPMENT CHECK LIST

_____ Batons for the relay races.

_____ Blank paper (lined).

_____ Blank shells (.32 caliber minimum).

_____ Brooms for field event runways, circles, etc.

_____ Chairs for field event officials.

_____ Chronomix or other multi-timing device.

_____ Clipboards.

_____ Crossbars.

_____ Distance sideline markers for the throwing events, if needed.

_____ Electric (automatic) photo-timer.

_____ Field event name indicator boards.

_____ Finish yarn.

_____ Flags for restraining ropes.

_____ Foul-fair flags (red and white) for Inspectors and field event officials.

_____ Friction tape.

_____ Hammers or mallets for starting blocks, etc.

_____ Hurdle line.

_____ Hurdles.

_____ Implements (shots, discuses, javelins, hammers).

_____ Implement scales.

_____ Ladder (15 ft.) for pole vault.

_____ Landing pits.

_____ Lap counter.

_____ "Last lap" bell.

_____ Masking tape.

_____ Megaphone or bull-horn.

_____ Name cards (for Name Indicator Boards), plus numbers for rounds and marks.

_____ Officials' stands (for finish judges and timers).

_____ Pencils and pens.

_____ Plasticine or other foul-detection substance.

_____ Rakes, level board.

_____ Restraining ropes.

_____ Rubber bands.

_____ Rule books.

_____ Safety pins, numbers.

_____ Score sheets and event cards.

_____ Sector flags.

_____ Shovels.

_____ Spikes and spike wrench.

_____ Standards for high jump and pole vault.

_____ Starter's pistols (.32 caliber minimum).

_____ Starting block carrier (or wheelbarrow).

_____ Starting blocks.

_____ Steel tapes (meters and feet—50, 100, 300 ft.).

_____ Stop watches.

_____ Vaulting poles and rack.

_____ Walkie talkies.

_____ Whistles.

_____ Wind gauges.

SPECIALS (TRAINER'S SUPPLIES)

_____ Ace bandages.   _____ Heel cups.

_____ Adhesive tape.   _____ Ice and ice bags.

_____ Alcohol.   _____ Laces (for shoes).

_____ Balms.   _____ Lemons, oranges, etc.

_____ Band-aids, bandages.   _____ Towels and blankets.

_____ Cups (paper).   _____ Water and water cooler.

_____ First Aid Kit

PERSONNEL CHECK LIST

List the names of the following working crews and post it on the track bulletin board the day before the track meet:

A) *Hurdle Crew:*

1. _____   6. _____

2. _____   7. _____

3. _____   8. _____

4. _____   9. _____

5. _____   10. _____

B) *Starting Block Crew (4 are plenty for a field of 8 lanes):*

1. _____   3. _____

2. _____   4. _____

C) *Finish Tape Attendants:*

1. _____   2. _____

D) *Messengers For The Coaches and Officials:*

1. _____ 6. _____
2. _____ 7. _____
3. _____ 8. _____
4. _____ 9. _____
5. _____ 10. _____

E) *Managers (Assistants):*

1. _____ 6. _____
2. _____ 7. _____
3. _____ 8. _____
4. _____ 9. _____
5. _____ 10. _____

F) *Attendants For the Visiting Track Team:*

1. _____ 2. _____

CONCLUSION OF THE TRACK MEET

Head Manager's Duties:

1. Have all the Assistant Managers assemble the equipment at the conclusion of the meet.
2. Check in all uniforms and track equipment.
3. Collect the meet results from the officials.
4. Furnish each track coach a copy of the meet results.
5. Record the results of the track meet.
6. Notify the newspapers of the meet results.
7. List the expenditures incurred for the meet.
8. Submit a budget report of expenses (for away meets) to the Head Track Coach.
9. Write a brief and factual report of the away track meet (or home meet).

OFFICIALS' ASSIGNMENT SHEET

Track Meet: _____

_____ VS _____

Date: _____ Time: _____

Official's Assignment:	Name:	Stationed Area:
Referee	_____	_____
Starter	_____	_____
Recall Starter	_____	_____
Announcer	_____	_____
Assistant Announcers	1._____	_____
	2._____	_____
	3._____	_____
Messengers For The Announcer	1._____	_____
	2._____	_____
	3._____	_____
	4._____	_____
	5._____	_____
Recorders and Scorers	1._____	_____
	2._____	_____
Head Clerk Of The Course	_____	_____
Assistant Clerks Of The Course	1._____	_____
	2._____	_____
	3._____	_____

Head Finish Judge   _____   _____

Assistant Finish   *Name:*   *Place Picking:*
Judges

	Name:	Place Picking:
1.	_____	First Place
2.	_____	First Place
3.	_____	Second Place
4.	_____	Second Place
5.	_____	Third Place
6.	_____	Third Place
7.	_____	Fourth Place
8.	_____	Fourth Place
9.	_____	Fifth Place
10.	_____	Fifth Place
11.	_____	Sixth Place
12.	_____	Sixth Place
13.	_____	Seventh Place
14.	_____	Seventh Place
15.	_____	Eighth Place
16.	_____	Eighth Place

Head Timer   _____   _____

Assistant Timers

	Name:	Place Picking:
1.	_____	First Place
2.	_____	First Place
3.	_____	First Place
4.	_____	First Place (Alternate)
5.	_____	Second Place
6.	_____	Second Place
7.	_____	Third Place
8.	_____	Third Place
9.	_____	Fourth Place
10.	_____	Fourth Place
11.	_____	Fifth Place

12._____	Sixth Place
13._____	Seventh Place
14._____	Eighth Place

Head Shot Put
Official   _____   _____

Assistant Shot Put
Officials   1._____   _____
                  2._____   _____
                  3._____   _____
                  4._____   _____
                  5._____   _____
                  6._____   _____
                  7._____   _____
                  8._____   _____

Head Discus Official   _____   _____

Assistant Discus
Officials   1._____   _____
                  2._____   _____
                  3._____   _____
                  4._____   _____
                  5._____   _____
                  6._____   _____
                  7._____   _____
                  8._____   _____

Head Hammer
Official   _____   _____

Assistant Hammer
Officials   1._____   _____

2._____   _____
3._____   _____
4._____   _____
5._____   _____
6._____   _____
7._____   _____
8._____   _____
9._____   _____

Head Javelin
Official   _____   _____

Assistant Javelin
Officials
1._____   _____
2._____   _____
3._____   _____
4._____   _____
5._____   _____
6._____   _____
7._____   _____
8._____   _____
9._____   _____

Head Pole Vault
Official   _____   _____

Assistant Pole Vault
Officials
1._____   _____
2._____   _____
3._____   _____
4._____   _____
5._____   _____
6._____   _____

Head High Jump
 Official   _____   _____

Assistant High Jump
 Officials   1._____   _____
               2._____   _____
               3._____   _____
               4._____   _____
               5._____   _____
               6._____   _____
               7._____   _____

Head Long Jump
 Official   _____   _____

Assistant Long Jump
 Officials   1._____   _____
               2._____   _____
               3._____   _____
               4._____   _____
               5._____   _____
               6._____   _____
               7._____   _____
               8._____   _____

Head Triple Jump
 Official   _____   _____

Assistant Triple Jump
 Officials   1._____   _____
               2._____   _____
               3._____   _____
               4._____   _____
               5._____   _____

	6._____	_____
	7._____	_____
	8._____	_____

Head Field Official	_____	_____
Head Inspector	_____	_____
Assistant Inspectors	1._____	Turn I
	2._____	Turn II
	3._____	Turn III
	4._____	Turn IV
	5._____	Back-Stretch
	6._____	Home-Stretch
	7._____	Turn 1B
	8._____	Turn 2B
Finish Tape Holders	1._____	_____
	2._____	_____

WORKING CREW

	Name:	Area:
Starting Blocks Crew:	1._____	_____
	2._____	_____
	3._____	_____
	4._____	_____
Hurdle Crew:	1._____	_____
	2._____	_____
	3._____	_____

4._____ _____
5._____ _____
6._____ _____
7._____ _____
8._____ _____
9._____ _____
10._____ _____

Head Manager: _____ _____

Managers:
(Assistants)
1._____ _____
2._____ _____
3._____ _____
4._____ _____
5._____ _____
6._____ _____
7._____ _____
8._____ _____

Attendants For
The Visiting Team:
1._____ _____
2._____ _____

Messengers For
The Coaches:
1._____ _____
2._____ _____
3._____ _____
4._____ _____
5._____ _____

MANAGER'S ASSIGNMENT SHEET

DAY OF THE TRACK MEET

Meet: _____

_____ VS _____

Date: _____ Time: _____

Hurdle Crew: *Name:*   *Hurdle Flight:*

                         1._____   _____

                         2._____   _____

                         3._____   _____

                         4._____   _____

                         5._____   _____

                         6._____   _____

                         7._____   _____

                         8._____   _____

                         9._____   _____

                        10._____   _____

Starting Blocks
Crew (Head):   _____

Starting Blocks
Crew (Assistants): 1._____   _____

                         2._____   _____

                         3._____   _____

                         4._____   _____

STARTING BLOCK ATTENDANTS

1. Set starting blocks for each competitor.
2. Use wooden mallets to pound the pins in securely—(for dirt tracks).
3. Loosen the wing-nuts of the starting blocks.
4. Do not leave any mallets or hammers near the area.
5. After the starting blocks have been placed, stay quite a distance from the starting line.
6. When the competitors have left the blocks, remove and get the starting blocks to the next starting area.
7. Use a wheel-barrow or a starting block carrier to transport the starting blocks to another area.
8. Make sure each starting block is in good working order.
9. Return the starting blocks to the equipment shack after the track meet has been concluded and stack them in the proper place.

Finish Tape
   Attendants: 1._____   _____

                        2._____   _____

Long/Triple Jump Crew (to level pits):

                        1._____   _____

                        2._____   _____

                        3._____   _____

Messengers For
   The Coaches: 1._____   _____

                        2._____   _____

                        3._____   _____

Sweat Suit
   Attendants: 1._____   _____

                        2._____   _____

                        3._____   _____

                        4._____   _____

Name Boards
Crew (Head): _____

Name Boards
Crew (Attendants):

        1. Discus _____ _____

        2. High Jump _____ _____

        3. Javelin _____ _____

        4. Long Jump _____ _____

        5. Pole Vault _____ _____

        6. Shot Put _____ _____

        7. Triple Jump _____ _____

        8. Hammer _____ _____

Manager (Head): _____

Managers (Assistants):

             Name: *Area:*

        1. _____ _____

        2. _____ _____

        3. _____ _____

        4. _____ _____

        5. _____ _____

TRACK MARKINGS

1. Place permanent plates for the "Start" and the "Finish" for each running event. (It is recommended that the finish of each race end at the same finish line.)
2. Markings may be placed:
   A) On the fence.
   B) On the wall.
   C) Embedded on the curb.
   D) On planted poles.
3. Track markings aid the Clerk of the Course and the athletes.

IMPORTANT ADDRESSES
AND RESOURCES

National Federation of State High School Associations
11724 Plaza Circle, P.O. Box 20626, Kansas City, MO 64195

National Collegiate Athletic Association
U.S. Highway 50 and Nall Avenue, P.O. Box 1906, Shawnee Mission, KS 66222

National Association of Intercollegiate Athletics
1221 Baltimore, Kansas City, MO 64105

Association For Intercollegiate Athletics For Women
1201 16th Street N.W., Washington, DC 20036

National Junior College Athletic Association
P.O. Box 10636, Hutchinson, KS 67501

Wilkins International (Track marking)
1145 Rolling Green Drive, Waukesha, WI 53186

International Amateur Athletic Federation
162 Upper Richmond Road
Putney, London SW15 2SL, England

Chronomix Corporation
650F Vaqueros Avenue, Sunnyvale, CA 94086

International Dictating Equipment, Inc.
Airport International Plaza
125 Wilbur Place, Bohemia, NY 11716

Research Engineering Corporation (Electronic Wind Gauge)
Morrisville, VT 05661

The Athletics Congress/U.S.A.
P.O. Box 120, Indianapolis, IN 46206

Track & Field News (Metric Conversion Book)
Box 296, Los Altos, CA 94022

Athletic Score Book Company
1595 Los Osos Valley Road 15C
Los Osos, CA 93402